OPPOSING
VIEWPOINTS®
SERIES

Reforming Wall Street

Other Books of Related Interest:

Opposing Viewpoints Series

Election Spending

For-Profit Education

Welfare

At Issue Series

Are Executives Paid Too Much?

Corporate Corruption

Current Controversies Series

Government Corruption

The Tea Party Movement

"Congress shall make no law . . . abridging the freedom of speech, or of the press."

First Amendment to the US Constitution

The basic foundation of our democracy is the First Amendment guarantee of freedom of expression. The *Opposing Viewpoints* series is dedicated to the concept of this basic freedom and the idea that it is more important to practice it than to enshrine it.

Reforming Wall Street

David Haugen and Susan Musser, Book Editors

GREENHAVEN PRESS
A part of Gale, Cengage Learning

GALE
CENGAGE Learning

Detroit • New York • San Francisco • New Haven, Conn • Waterville, Maine • London

Christine Nasso, *Publisher*
Elizabeth Des Chenes, *Managing Editor*

© 2011 Greenhaven Press, a part of Gale, Cengage Learning

Gale and Greenhaven Press are registered trademarks used herein under license.

For more information, contact:
Greenhaven Press
27500 Drake Rd.
Farmington Hills, MI 48331-3535
Or you can visit our Internet site at gale.cengage.com

Articles in Greenhaven Press anthologies are often edited for length to meet page require-ments. In addition, original titles of these works are changed to clearly present the main thesis and to explicitly indicate the author's opinion. Every effort is made to ensure that Greenhaven Press accurately reflects the original intent of the authors. Every effort has been made to trace the owners of copyrighted material.

Cover image copyright © Karen To/Flickr/Getty Images.

LIBRARY OF CONGRESS CATALOGING-IN-PUBLICATION DATA

Reforming Wall Street / David Haugen and Susan Musser, book editors.
    p. cm. -- (Opposing viewpoints)
    Includes bibliographical references and index.
    ISBN 978-0-7377-5235-9 (hardcover) -- ISBN 978-0-7377-5236-6 (pbk.)
    1. Financial crises--United States--21st century. 2. Global Financial Crisis, 2008-2009. 3. Financial institutions--Law and legislation--United States. I. Haugen, David M., 1969- II. Musser, Susan.
    HB3722.R427 2011
    332.0973--dc22
                                                                    2010044351

Printed in the United States of America
1 2 3 4 5 6 7 15 14 13 12 11

Contents

Chapter 3: Will Financial Reform Legislation Be Effective?

Why Consider Opposing Viewpoints?

> *"The only way in which a human being can make some approach to knowing the whole of a subject is by hearing what can be said about it by persons of every variety of opinion and studying all modes in which it can be looked at by every character of mind. No wise man ever acquired his wisdom in any mode but this."*
>
> *John Stuart Mill*

In our media-intensive culture it is not difficult to find differing opinions. Thousands of newspapers and magazines and dozens of radio and television talk shows resound with differing points of view. The difficulty lies in deciding which opinion to agree with and which "experts" seem the most credible. The more inundated we become with differing opinions and claims, the more essential it is to hone critical reading and thinking skills to evaluate these ideas. Opposing Viewpoints books address this problem directly by presenting stimulating debates that can be used to enhance and teach these skills. The varied opinions contained in each book examine many different aspects of a single issue. While examining these conveniently edited opposing views, readers can develop critical thinking skills such as the ability to compare and contrast authors' credibility, facts, argumentation styles, use of persuasive techniques, and other stylistic tools. In short, the Opposing Viewpoints Series is an ideal way to attain the higher-level thinking and reading skills so essential in a culture of diverse and contradictory opinions.

In addition to providing a tool for critical thinking, *Opposing Viewpoints* books challenge readers to question their own strongly held opinions and assumptions. Most people form their opinions on the basis of upbringing, peer pressure, and personal, cultural, or professional bias. By reading carefully balanced opposing views, readers must directly confront new ideas as well as the opinions of those with whom they disagree. This is not to argue simplistically that everyone who reads opposing views will—or should—change his or her opinion. Instead, the series enhances readers' understanding of their own views by encouraging confrontation with opposing ideas. Careful examination of others' views can lead to the readers' understanding of the logical inconsistencies in their own opinions, perspective on why they hold an opinion, and the consideration of the possibility that their opinion requires further evaluation.

Evaluating Other Opinions

To ensure that this type of examination occurs, *Opposing Viewpoints* books present all types of opinions. Prominent spokespeople on different sides of each issue as well as well-known professionals from many disciplines challenge the reader. An additional goal of the series is to provide a forum for other, less known, or even unpopular viewpoints. The opinion of an ordinary person who has had to make the decision to cut off life support from a terminally ill relative, for example, may be just as valuable and provide just as much insight as a medical ethicist's professional opinion. The editors have two additional purposes in including these less known views. One, the editors encourage readers to respect others' opinions—even when not enhanced by professional credibility. It is only by reading or listening to and objectively evaluating others' ideas that one can determine whether they are worthy of consideration. Two, the inclusion of such viewpoints encourages the important critical thinking skill of objectively evaluating an author's credentials and bias. This evaluation will illuminate an author's reasons for taking a particular stance on an issue and will aid in readers' evaluation of the author's ideas.

It is our hope that these books will give readers a deeper understanding of the issues debated and an appreciation of the complexity of even seemingly simple issues when good and honest people disagree. This awareness is particularly important in a democratic society such as ours in which people enter into public debate to determine the common good. Those with whom one disagrees should not be regarded as enemies but rather as people whose views deserve careful examination and may shed light on one's own.

Thomas Jefferson once said that "difference of opinion leads to inquiry, and inquiry to truth." Jefferson, a broadly educated man, argued that "if a nation expects to be ignorant and free . . . it expects what never was and never will be." As individuals and as a nation, it is imperative that we consider the opinions of others and examine them with skill and discernment. The *Opposing Viewpoints* series is intended to help readers achieve this goal.

David L. Bender and Bruno Leone,
Founders

Introduction

> *"There has always been a tension between the desire to allow markets to function without interference and the absolute necessity of rules to prevent markets from falling out of kilter. But managing that tension, one that we've debated since the founding of this nation, is what has allowed our country to keep up with a changing world. For in taking up this debate . . . we ensure that we don't tip too far one way or the other—that our democracy remains as dynamic and our economy remains as dynamic as it has in the past. So, yes, this debate can be contentious. It can be heated. But in the end it serves only to make our country stronger."*
>
> *—President Barack Obama,*
> *Remarks on Wall Street reform*
> *at Cooper Union, New York,*
> *April 22, 2010*

The financial crisis that began in 2008 was sparked by a collapse of the housing bubble that had been expanding for a decade. The growth of worldwide investment capital prompted large financial institutions to tap into the mortgage industry, which in turn was fueled by rampant home-buying in the United States. Traders on Wall Street packaged mortgages and sold them to eager buyers across the globe who wanted to cash in on the rising housing prices, and when supplies wore thin, banks began issuing substandard, or subprime, mortgages to keep feeding the demand. Eventually, the market caught up with demand and housing prices—which had been artificially inflated by easy mortgages—and, by 2008, the values dropped. The National Association of Realtors reported the following year that the median price of existing homes declined 12.4 percent in 2008. The bubble burst, and banks and investors hemorrhaged funds—capital they didn't always have because they often bought the mortgage-backed securities with little money down. New investors became skittish, and various markets saw catastrophic downturns. Writing for the Heritage Foundation, Ronald Utt explained, "The collapse . . . set in motion a chain reaction of economic and financial adversity that has spread to global financial markets, created depression-like conditions in the housing market, and pushed the US economy to the brink of recession."

In the midst of the crisis, many observers pointed fingers at Wall Street, the home of the banking institutions that had for so long reaped huge profits from mortgage trades but cried victim when the market collapsed. Dean Baker, economist and codirector of the Center for Economic and Policy Research in Washington, D.C., wrote a piece for the Campaign for America's Future website on September 15, 2008, in which he lambasted banking chief executive officers (CEOs) who ran their institutions into the ground while collecting huge salaries. "The bankers who messed up and destroyed the companies who hired them are still multimillionaires," Baker stated. "Most of them are still in their old jobs getting multimillion-dollar pay packages. This is a sector that badly cries out for reform and there is no better time than now to put it into place." The two presidential front-runners in the 2008 race also argued that the financial district needed more regulation. Arizona senator John McCain, the Republican candidate, was perhaps the most vocal in challenging the kind of unmonitored Wall Street speculation that he believed had brought the country to its knees. He told supporters in Orlando, Florida, that his election would "put an end . . . to running Wall Street like a casino."

Although Illinois senator Barack Obama won the presidency in 2008, McCain joined Senator Maria Cantwell of Washington in promoting a 2009 congressional bill aimed at separating commercial banks from investment banks so that the public's access to loans and other commercial products would not be affected if investment banks continued to "gamble" money on risky ventures. "It is time to put a stop to the taxpayer financed excesses of Wall Street," McCain said in a press release for the bill. McCain's rhetoric was echoed by many other critics—both liberal and conservative—who felt the country had been cheated when the federal government—under George W. Bush—had set aside tax money to shore up some of the big banks that had lost so much money in the collapse. If Wall Street business practices are to be reformed through legislation, they argued, then the government must craft legislation that lets huge banking firms fail if they risk too much. Most Republicans, however, worried that a reform measure would not stop there and that government would seek to regulate business—a proposition that bespoke the expansion of big government at the expense of economic freedom.

On February 25, 2009, President Obama ordered his financial advisers to begin coordinating legislation with Congress to initiate a financial reform bill. Treasury Secretary Timothy Geithner provided written testimony to the House Financial Services Committee hearing on the issue in which he stated, "Financial institutions and markets that are critical to the functioning of the financial system and that could pose serious risks to the stability of the financial system need to be subject to strong oversight by the government." Republican fears seemed justified. Sponsored by Democratic representative Barney Frank of Massachusetts, the reform bill that moved through the House of Representatives called for the creation of a council to oversee banking practices and to judge when a financial firm was in trouble and in need of dismantling. It also called for banks to hold onto more capital to insure against risks, and it forced banks to conduct securities trades through clearinghouses to ensure transparency and to provide investors with information about the risks they were taking by purchasing these securities. The House bill passed without support from Republicans, who accused the legislation of overreaching its aim. In June 2010, it was married to its sister bill in the Senate, sponsored by Democrat Chris Dodd of Connecticut. After some revisions, the joint Dodd-Frank Wall Street Reform and Consumer Protection Act became law on July 21, 2010. Upon signing the bill, President Obama remarked, "For years, our financial sector was governed by antiquated and poorly enforced rules that allowed some to game the system and take risks that endangered the entire economy. . . . [This new law] demands accountability and responsibility from everyone. It provides certainty to everybody, from bankers to farmers to business owners to consumers. And unless your business model depends on cutting corners or bilking your customers, you've got nothing to fear from reform."

Not everyone heralded the new law. Some argue the intrusion of government into the affairs of business—especially demanding that banks hold more capital and restrict certain profitable trading enterprises—likely means that financial institutions will tighten lending practices to small businesses and likewise curtail consumer credit. This could mean that businesses will lack the capital to hire more employees or make investments in growth. House Republican Mike Pence of Indiana issued a statement—just days before the signing—in which he claimed, "This bill can be summed up in two words: 'government control,' and it will serve as the latest piece of the president's job-killing agenda." Furthermore, critics are dismayed that the bill does nothing to rein in the excesses of the Federal Home Loan Mortgage Corporation (Freddie Mac) or the Federal National Mortgage Association (Fannie Mae), two government-sponsored enterprises that encouraged the spread of subprime loans to increase housing affordability to low-income Americans. These organizations also traded in mortgage bundles and have been receiving taxpayer bailout funds to keep them viable. Because Congress is keen to let large investment banks fail, critics wonder why the government is not willing to apply the same logic to its own mortgage companies.

In *Opposing Viewpoints: Reforming Wall Street,* many of the most vocal advocates and detractors debate the need for greater banking regulation. In chapters titled Does Wall Street Need Financial Reform? and Will Financial Reform Legislation Be Effective? these legislators, economists, and pundits air their views on proposed elements of the legislation and the impact reform will have on the economy. Other analysts provide background controversies in an initial chapter titled What Caused the Financial Crisis? As the articles in this anthology attest, these debates have occupied much media attention since the financial collapse in 2008. As some writers have noted, however, the economy has shown only signs of slow recovery in 2010, and more Americans are worried about unemployment and mortgage rates than about reining in Wall Street. "It has yet to play out and affect the lives of Americans," Ross Baker, a Rutgers political scientist, told a July 18, 2010, Reuters reporter. "For now," the Reuters report continued, "the jobless rate, which stands at 9.5 percent, trumps . . . financial reform."

What Caused the Financial Crisis?

Chapter Preface

Between 2005 and 2006 the housing market in the United States peaked. Home prices had risen steadily for several years (around 12.5 percent in 2005 alone), and several analysts warned that the accelerated growth was forming a bubble that would soon pop. When it did, real estate values dropped precipitously. Overvalued homes lost more than 5 percent of their value in 2006, but worse for many homeowners, the fall in value meant that banks had to readjust their mortgage rates.

Since the 1990s, millions of Americans had purchased their homes at subprime rates, meaning the buyers had less-than-ideal credit and could put little money down to finance properties. When the market was soaring, banks were willing to make such low-interest deals because they could package these mortgages and sell them as securities to hedge their risk. Government-sponsored mortgage enterprises prompted banks to make subprime loans because these institutions were given tax incentives to buy up the mortgage securities. When the housing market began its decline, banks raised their interest rates on the subprime loans, and high-risk borrowers found they could neither refinance nor make their mortgage payments. RealtyTrac, an online source for foreclosure information, reported that more than 3 million foreclosure filings occurred in 2008, an 81 percent increase over 2007 filings, which were 79 percent higher than in 2006.

With foreclosures up and home prices down, the value of the real estate–backed securities plummeted. Wall Street financial organizations such as Citigroup, Bank of America, and JP-Morgan Chase that traded in these securities lost billions of dollars, and to shore up their holdings, they began restricting credit to consumers. Cutting credit lines curtailed public spending, and the economy slowed remarkably. The shock was felt throughout the world not only because other nations rely on US consumer health but also because the toxic securities had been bought up by foreign investors as well. In 2010 the International Monetary Fund fixed the global losses from bad loans and depreciated or worthless assets at $2.28 trillion, of which roughly $885 billion was held by US financial institutions.

At home, the crisis was amplified by rising oil prices and a not-unexpected downturn in the construction and home maintenance industries. Other companies began laying off workers to make up for bad investments and the lack of consumer spending. To stave off complete financial collapse, the government under George W. Bush created the Troubled Asset Relief Program (TARP) to buy up bad securities. The government essentially lent banks $245 billion to cover their losses and keep several key institutions from failing. This bailout has remained controversial, as it demonstrated the government's willingness to save banks that had essentially overspeculated on an unsound market. As Matthew Jaffe reported on the ABC News website on October 3, 2009, "Supporters say the program pulled the financial system back from the brink of disaster. . . . Detractors counter by arguing that the program only rewarded Wall Street, the same institutions blamed for causing the mess in the first place."

In the following chapter, various analysts and commentators examine whether Wall Street gambling was indeed the cause of the financial crisis or whether other system-wide problems allowed—even encouraged—the reckless speculation that many people believe is at the heart of the disaster.

> *"Obama laid blame for the financial crisis squarely at the feet of the banks, railed against their 'excess and abuse,' and laid out far-reaching new regulations on them."*

Wall Street Is to Blame for the Financial Crisis

Charles Hurt and David Seifman

In the following viewpoint, Charles Hurt and David Seifman discuss President Barack Obama's all-out war on Wall Street. Obama believes that Wall Street and its investment banks took risks and used "excess and abuse" to bring about the financial crisis. The president communicates his resolve to reform the banks and industry he believes caused the crisis by ensuring that Wall Street pays back the American people for the bailout. Charles Hurt and David Seifman are columnists for the New York Post.

As you read, consider the following questions:

1. According to the article, what would the proposed reforms give the federal government?

2. What would the reforms force banks to get rid of?

Charles Hurt and David Seifman, "'Populist' Prez Bonks the Banks," *New York Post*, January 22, 2010. Reproduced by permission.

3. As stated in the article, which banks "would have to change radically or stop being banks"?

Striking a fighting populist stance in a bid to reverse his sagging political fortunes, President Obama yesterday portrayed himself as the champion of Main Street while unleashing an all-out war on Wall Street.

Obama laid blame for the financial crisis squarely at the feet of the banks, railed against their "excess and abuse," and laid out far-reaching new regulations on them that instantly drew sour reactions from [New York] Mayor [Michael] Bloomberg and others concerned about the vitality of the financial industry.

Speaking in sometimes fiery language two days after Republican Scott Brown's Senate win in Massachusetts altered the political landscape, Obama said he had welcomed input from the financial sector.

"But what we've seen so far, in recent weeks, is an army of industry lobbyists from Wall Street descending on Capitol Hill to try and block basic and commonsense rules of the road that would protect our economy and the American people," he said hotly.

Ready to Fight

"If these folks want a fight, it's a fight I'm ready to have," Obama said. "And my resolve is only strengthened when I see a return to old practices at some of the very firms fighting reform.

"We've come through a terrible crisis. The American people have paid a very high price," he said. "We simply cannot return to business as usual.

"That's why we're going to ensure that Wall Street pays back the American people for the bailout," said Obama, who approved much of the bailout. "That's why we're going to rein

---

Senator John McCain Accuses Banks of Excessive Self-Interest

Too many people on Wall Street have forgotten or disregarded the basic rules of sound finance. . . . They dreamed up investment schemes that they themselves don't even understand. With their derivatives, credit default swaps, and mortgage-backed securities they tried to make their own rules. But they could only avoid the basic rules of economics for so long.

John McCain,
"Prepared Remarks of McCain in Tampa, Florida,"
September 16, 2008. http://thepage.time.com.

---

in the excess and abuse that nearly brought down our financial system. That's why we're going to pass these reforms into law."

The proposed reforms would give the federal government the power to limit the size and activities of large financial institutions. The new rules, which need congressional approval, would force banks to get rid of their proprietary trading desks—meaning they cannot trade in financial markets for their own profit.

So-called prop desks are often among the most profitable areas at large banks like Citigroup and JPMorgan Chase—and investment banks like Goldman Sachs and Morgan Stanley would have to change radically or stop being banks.

Obama's plan drew harsh criticism from the markets, which tanked yesterday, and bank stocks fell so hard that the federal government itself lost $1.5 billion on the shares of Citigroup it owns.

"My recollection is that the big banks that got in trouble, most of them—Bear Stearns, Lehman, Merrill—those weren't commercial banks. Those were the investment banks," Bloomberg said. "So I don't know why that would really solve the problem."

And Bloomberg did not spare Congress.

"I just find it sort of ironic that congressmen, senators who make more than double what the average person working in finance makes," he said.

"They're the rich ones, and they're talking about trying to restrict bonuses and taxing the industries that are our lifeblood."

Tremendous Impact

Sen. Kirsten Gillibrand (D-NY) issued a statement supporting Obama's plan, saying, "If we hope to avert the type of catastrophic meltdown we witnessed last year, we must contain the levels of risk and activities the big banks undertake."

Sen. Charles Schumer (D-NY), Wall Street's protector in the past, had no comment.

The Dow Jones industrial average tumbled 210 points after dropping 122 on Wednesday.

Ralph Fogel, investment strategist at Fogel Neale Partners in New York, said of Obama's proposals: "This is going to have a tremendous impact on big-name brokerage firms. If they stop prop trading, it will not only dry up liquidity in the market, but it will change the whole structure of Wall Street."

| *"Your average Wall Street deal-maker couldn't get a loan on the terms that were routine in all of Southern California."*

Wall Street Is Not to Blame for the Financial Crisis

Mark Gimein

Mark Gimein is a reporter whose writing has appeared in the New York Times, New York Magazine, *and other popular publications. In the viewpoint that follows, Gimein asserts that Wall Street is unfairly demonized as the source of the current financial crisis. In Gimein's opinion, Wall Street banks did not finance risky mortgage deals that burst the housing bubble at the heart of the crisis; instead, he claims that most mortgages were transacted by bad lenders on the West Coast and other parts of America. Gimein states that Wall Street banks only ended up buying these loans and reselling them to spread risk—a proper course of action for these institutions.*

As you read, consider the following questions:

1. According to Gimein, what company came up with the negative-amortization mortgage?

Mark Gimein, "Shooting the Salesman," *New York Magazine*, October 5, 2008. Reprinted with permission.

2. In the bundle of 2007 Washington Mutual mortgages tracked by blogger Michael Shedlock, what percentage of these loans went bad in less than two years?

3. In what way does Gimein compare Wall Street to a salesman?

In the midst of the financial crisis, the country is at least able to reach bipartisan agreement on where to fix the blame: Wall Street. It is a convenient explanation for voters wanting to be reassured that someone else is at fault, but it is starting to look unconvincing, or at least badly incomplete. Because at the bottom of the muck-filled well of the banking collapse lies something much simpler than the complicated bonds and derivatives that are Wall Street's stock-in-trade: bad loans. Really, really bad loans.

Bad Lenders That Are Not on Wall Street

New York is supposed to be the world capital of financial sophistication, but when it comes to the Rube Goldberg [overly complicated] contrivances that kept the real estate market going in California, Florida, and other parts of the country, we are duffers. To the average, or even not-so-average, New Yorker, the mortgage-speak that is familiar to folks who bought houses in places like San Diego—"negative amortization," "alternative/reduced documentation"—is gibberish. If you want to find the birthplace of the depraved mortgage culture, you can go to Oakland, California, the headquarters of Golden West (bought by Wachovia and the source of its troubles), the people who invented the negative-amortization mortgage—a mortgage on which you pay less than the interest for a few years, until the payments rise and you either refinance or move out. Or maybe to Seattle, the headquarters of Washington Mutual [WaMu], which might have set the standard for bad lending. One financial analyst and blogger named Michael Shedlock kept a monthly tally of the loans going bad in one bundle of Washington Mutual mortgages from 2007 (yes, that's last year). In the post-Depression era, no more than 2 or 3 percent of all mortgages have failed in a year. After less than two years, half of this batch of WaMu loans had soured or were at least two months behind.

It was not Wall Street that gave home buyers mellifluous assurances. In fact, the culture of New York lending and the co-op rules that imposed an extra (and, it's now obvious, useful) level of restraint on real estate in New York meant that your average Wall Street deal-maker couldn't get a loan on the terms that were routine in all of Southern California.

Hiding the Source of Bad Loans

So where did Wall Street come in? The investment houses did what their job is in any bubble: They sold it to their clients. The hundreds of billions of dollars of shoddy loans that mortgage underwriters made were packaged off and retailed to investors around the world. Not all the loans: The banks kept plenty on their own books—if they could have gotten rid of them all, Wachovia and Washington Mutual and Countrywide would still be in business. But many, many billions of dollars of them were bundled, cut up into slices to make "mortgage-backed securities" and "CDOs" [collateralized debt obligations] and an alphabet soup of other bonds.

The mystique of Wall Street is all about the knowledge business. But the reality has been that most of it is about the sales business, putting its imprimatur on investments and in the process, especially in the later stage of a bubble, rubbing away the marks of their less-than-pristine origins. And by doing so, Wall Street shields the rest of the market from responsibility. We have seen the pattern before. The junk-bond frenzy will forever be linked with the names Ivan Boesky and Michael Milken [businessmen indicted for insider trading and junk bond sales in the 1980s]. We remember that the savings and loan crisis took down Salomon Brothers; who can recall the banks involved? And when it came to the indigestion that followed the Internet smorgasbord, it was the investment banks that walked into court for a round robin of fines, not the Silicon Valley executives or the venture capitalists who'd cashed in their shares as their dot-coms cratered.

This may be the death of Wall Street as we know it. But rest assured that when the next speculative frenzy comes around, someone will be there to retail it, whether it's called Wall Street or something else.

> "The poor choices of these two government-sponsored enterprises (GSEs)—and their sponsors in Washington—are largely to blame for our current mess."

Government Mortgage Practices Are Largely Responsible for the Financial Crisis

Charles W. Calomiris and Peter J. Wallison

In the following viewpoint, Charles W. Calomiris and Peter J. Wallison claim that the government-sponsored loan enterprises Fannie Mae (Federal National Mortgage Association) and Freddie Mac (Federal Home Loan Mortgage Corporation) are largely responsible for the financial crisis that began in 2008. According to to the authors, these institutions started buying up risky subprime mortgages to build a reputation as the champions of affordable housing. Despite the warnings of some critics, Fannie Mae and Freddie Mac took on more risk than they could handle, and their zeal also prompted other banking firms to gamble ex-

Charles W. Calomiris and Peter J. Wallison, "Blame Fannie Mae and Congress for the Credit Mess," *Wall Street Journal*, September 23, 2008. Reprinted with permission.

cessively in the subprime market, Calomiris and Wallison attest. Furthermore, the authors insist that the eventual collapse of the market would have been less devastating if congressional Democrats had not blindly supported Fannie Mae and Freddie Mac and had instead given in to Republican calls for reform. Charles W. Calomiris is a professor of finance and economics at Columbia Business School and a scholar at the American Enterprise Institute for Public Policy Research (AEI). Peter J. Wallison, a senior fellow at AEI, was general counsel of the Treasury Department in the Ronald Reagan administration.

As you read, consider the following questions:

1. Why were Fannie Mae and Freddie Mac allowed to borrow so much capital to buy mortgages, according to Calomiris and Wallison?

2. As the authors report, what percentage of all mortgages were subprime mortgages in 2006?

3. Why do Calomiris and Wallison reject the notion that deregulation was to blame for the financial crisis?

Many monumental errors and misjudgments contributed to the acute financial turmoil in which we now find ourselves. Nevertheless, the vast accumulation of toxic mortgage debt that poisoned the global financial system was driven by the aggressive buying of subprime and Alt-A mortgages [Alternative A-paper mortgages, issued to borrowers with lower credit scores or incomplete documentation], and mortgage-backed securities, by Fannie Mae [Federal National Mortgage Association] and Freddie Mac [Federal Home Loan Mortgage Corporation]. The poor choices of these two government-sponsored enterprises (GSEs)—and their sponsors in Washington—are largely to blame for our current mess.

Going After Subprime Loans

How did we get here? Let's review: In order to curry congressional support after their accounting scandals in 2003 and 2004, Fannie Mae and Freddie Mac committed to increased financing of "affordable housing." They became the largest buyers of subprime and Alt-A mortgages between 2004 and 2007, with total GSE exposure eventually exceeding $1 trillion. In doing so, they stimulated the growth of the subpar mortgage market and substantially magnified the costs of its collapse.

It is important to understand that, as GSEs, Fannie and Freddie were viewed in the capital markets as government-backed buyers (a belief that has now been reduced to fact). Thus they were able to borrow as much as they wanted for the purpose of buying mortgages and mortgage-backed securities. Their buying patterns and interests were followed closely in the markets. If Fannie and Freddie wanted subprime or Alt-A loans, the mortgage markets would produce them. By late 2004, Fannie and Freddie very much wanted subprime and Alt-A loans. Their accounting had just been revealed as fraudulent, and they were under pressure from Congress to demonstrate that they deserved their considerable privileges. Among other problems, economists at the Federal Reserve [Fed] and Congressional Budget Office had begun to study them in detail, and found that—despite their subsidized borrowing rates—they did not significantly reduce mortgage interest rates. In the wake of Freddie's 2003 accounting scandal, Fed Chairman Alan Greenspan became a powerful opponent, and began to call for stricter regulation of the GSEs and limitations on the growth of their highly profitable, but risky, retained portfolios.

If they were not making mortgages cheaper and were creating risks for the taxpayers and the economy, what value *were* they providing? The answer was their affordable-housing mission. So it was that, beginning in 2004, their portfolios of subprime and Alt-A loans and securities began to grow.

Federal Backing Allowed Freddie Mac and Fannie Mae to Grow Beyond the Limits of Their Capital

Congress was repeatedly warned by credible observers about the growing dangers posed by Fannie Mae's and Freddie Mac's implicit federal backing. A leading critic was William Poole, then president of the Federal Reserve Bank of St. Louis, who as far back as 2003 pointedly warned that the companies had insufficient capital to survive adverse conditions, and that the problem would continue to fester unless Congress explicitly removed the federal backing from the two companies so that they would face market discipline.

Congress did nothing. Efforts to rein in Fannie and Freddie came to naught because the two giants had cultivated powerful friends on Capitol Hill.

Lawrence H. White,
"How Did We Get into This Financial Mess?"
Cato Institute Briefing Papers, no. 110, November 18, 2008.

Subprime and Alt-A originations in the U.S. rose from less than 8% of all mortgages in 2003 to over 20% in 2006. During this period the quality of subprime loans also declined, going from fixed-rate, long-term amortizing loans to loans with low down payments and low (but adjustable) initial rates, indicating that originators were scraping the bottom of the barrel to find product for buyers like the GSEs.

Winning Congressional Support

The strategy of presenting themselves to Congress as the champions of affordable housing appears to have worked. Fannie and Freddie retained the support of many in Congress, particularly Democrats, and they were allowed to continue unrestrained. Rep. Barney Frank (D, Mass.), for example, now the chair of the House Financial Services Committee, openly described the "arrangement" with the GSEs at a committee hearing on GSE reform in 2003: "Fannie Mae and Freddie Mac have played a very useful role in helping to make housing more affordable . . . a mission that this Congress has given them in return for some of the arrangements which are of some benefit to them to focus on affordable housing." The hint to Fannie and Freddie was obvious: Concentrate on affordable housing and, despite your problems, your congressional support is secure.

In light of the collapse of Fannie and Freddie, both John McCain and Barack Obama [the 2008 Republican and Democratic presidential candidates, respectively] now criticize the risk-tolerant regulatory regime that produced the current crisis. But Sen. McCain's criticisms are at least credible, since he has been pointing to systemic risks in the mortgage market and trying to do something about them for years. In contrast, Sen. Obama's conversion as a financial reformer marks a reversal from his actions in previous years, when he did nothing to disturb the status quo. The first head of Mr. Obama's vice presidential search committee, Jim Johnson, a former chairman of Fannie Mae, was the one who announced Fannie's original affordable-housing program in 1991—just as Congress was taking up the first GSE regulatory legislation.

In 2005, the Senate Committee [on Banking, Housing, and Urban Affairs], then under Republican control, adopted a strong reform bill, introduced by Republican Sens. Elizabeth Dole, John Sununu and Chuck Hagel, and supported by then chairman Richard Shelby. The bill prohibited the GSEs from holding portfolios, and gave their regulator prudential authority (such as setting capital requirements) roughly equivalent to a bank regulator. In light of the current financial crisis, this bill was probably the most important piece of financial regulation before Congress in 2005 and 2006. All the Republicans on the committee supported the bill, and all the Democrats voted against it. Mr. McCain endorsed the legislation in a speech on the Senate floor. Mr. Obama, like all other Democrats, remained silent.

Deregulation Was Not the Culprit

Now the Democrats are blaming the financial crisis on "deregulation." This is a canard. There has indeed been deregulation in our economy—in long-distance telephone rates, airline fares, securities brokerage and trucking, to name just a few—and this has produced much innovation and lower consumer prices. But the primary "deregulation" in the financial world in the last 30 years permitted banks to diversify their risks geographically and across different products, which is one of the things that has kept banks relatively stable in this storm.

As a result, U.S. commercial banks have been able to attract more than $100 billion of new capital in the past year to replace most of their subprime-related write-downs. Deregulation of branching restrictions and limitations on bank product offerings also made possible bank acquisition of Bear Stearns and Merrill Lynch, saving billions in likely resolution costs for taxpayers.

If the Democrats had let the 2005 legislation come to a vote, the huge growth in the subprime and Alt-A loan portfolios of Fannie and Freddie could not have occurred, and the scale of the financial meltdown would have been substantially less. The same politicians who today decry the lack of intervention to stop excess risk taking in 2005–2006 were the ones who blocked the only legislative effort that could have stopped it.

"It is important to remember that Freddie [Mac], and its sister institution, Fannie Mae, did not create the subprime market."

Government Mortgage Practices Are Unfairly Blamed for the Financial Crisis

Richard F. Syron

In the following viewpoint, Richard F. Syron, a former chief executive officer of the Federal Home Loan Mortgage Corporation (Freddie Mac), maintains that the government-sponsored loan enterprises known as Freddie Mac and Fannie Mae (Federal National Mortgage Association) are not to blame for the subprime market collapse that caused the financial crisis in 2008. According to Syron, these institutions were mandated by Congress to provide affordable housing to Americans, and to do so, Freddie Mac and Fannie Mae had to deal in subprime mortgages because banks were already offering these less-than-perfect loans to home buyers.

Richard F. Syron, Statement Before the Committee on Oversight and Government Reform, United States House of Representatives, December 9, 2008. http://oversight.house.gov.

As you read, consider the following questions:

1. What are the first two factors that Syron claims contributed greatly to the collapse of the housing market?

2. According to Syron, why were the pressures on Freddie Mac and Fannie Mae so enormous when the housing market began its decline?

3. How did the delinquency and default rates of the GSEs compare to other institutions in the market when the market collapsed?

Let me start with a very basic proposition: Freddie Mac [Federal Home Loan Mortgage Corporation] was, is, and—by law—must be, a nondiversified financial services company, limited to the business of residential mortgages. Given the recent severe, nationwide downturn in the housing market—the only nationwide decline in home values since the Great Depression—any company limited exclusively to that line of business alone would be severely impacted. As Treasury Secretary [Henry] Paulson recently noted, given that the GSEs [government-sponsored enterprises] were "solely involved in housing," and given the "magnitude of the housing correction we've had," the losses by the GSEs should come as no surprise to anyone.

With respect to the housing market, the prolonged glut of credit certainly was one factor that contributed to the housing bubble and its subsequent collapse. Another important factor was the shift from a system in which the mortgage originators held loans to maturity, to a system in which mortgage originators immediately sold or securitized a loan and retained no risk. In more recent years, increasingly complex financial techniques were also applied to this process with the objective of minimizing, shifting, or—as some believed—virtually eliminating risk. We all recognize that homeownership provides benefits that generate substantial social advantages beyond

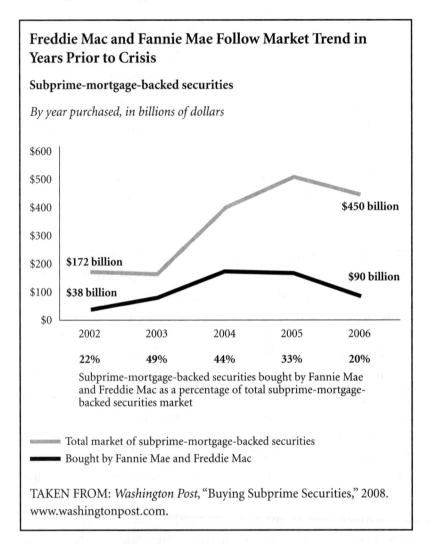

Freddie Mac and Fannie Mae Follow Market Trend in Years Prior to Crisis

Subprime-mortgage-backed securities

By year purchased, in billions of dollars

$172 billion

$38 billion

$450 billion

$90 billion

	2002	2003	2004	2005	2006
	22%	49%	44%	33%	20%

Subprime-mortgage-backed securities bought by Fannie Mae and Freddie Mac as a percentage of total subprime-mortgage-backed securities market

▬▬▬ Total market of subprime-mortgage-backed securities
━━━ Bought by Fannie Mae and Freddie Mac

TAKEN FROM: *Washington Post*, "Buying Subprime Securities," 2008. www.washingtonpost.com.

just shelter. We have learned the hard way, however, that rapid expansion of homeownership is not without risk and, ultimately, not without cost if the choices made by individual homeowners are unaffordable.

GSEs Were Hit Hard by the Crisis

What was the role of Fannie Mae and Freddie Mac in the credit crisis? These institutions were established by Congress to promote liquidity, affordability and stability in housing finance. They do so primarily by guaranteeing the timely payment of principal and interest on mortgages originated by banks in order to facilitate the purchase of those mortgages by institutional investors, thereby enabling banks to make new loans. Congress has reaffirmed this role for Fannie and Freddie many times, including quite recently. When the dramatic and widespread downturn in housing prices occurred, the pressures on Freddie Mac and Fannie Mae were enormous. The GSEs are in a nondiversified business focused solely on residential housing lending in the United States. As the guarantor of almost half the home mortgages in the country, it is not at all surprising that these two firms would get hit hard by the biggest housing collapse in 75 years. This lack of diversification was extremely challenging for the GSEs, even though their credit standards were tighter than other lenders.

Freddie Mac and Fannie Mae Followed a Market Trend

There has been a lot of attention in the media and elsewhere to problems associated with the nontraditional or "subprime" market. And, there is no question that Freddie Mac has incurred losses associated with nontraditional loans. But, it is important to remember that Freddie, and its sister institution, Fannie Mae, did not create the subprime market. Freddie was in fact a late entrant into nontraditional (i.e., non-30-year fixed interest/traditional underwriting) markets, such as Alt-A [Alternative A-paper mortgages, issued to borrowers with lower credit scores or incomplete documentation]. The subprime market was developed largely by private label participants, as were most nontraditional mortgage products. Freddie Mac entered the nontraditional slice of the market because, as the private lending sector shifted toward those types of loans, Freddie needed to participate in order to carry out its public mission of promoting affordability, liquidity and stability in housing finance. In addition, if it had not done so, it could not have remained competitive or even relevant in the residential mortgage market we were designed to serve. Moreover, if you are going to take the mission of promoting low-income lending seriously, then you are, by definition, going to take on a somewhat greater level of risk.

Freddie's delinquency rates and default rates, both overall and for each type of loan, were much lower than those of the market overall and were especially lower than for mortgages underwritten by purely private institutions—many of which were severely impaired for some of the same reasons as Fannie and Freddie. Every institution with significant exposure to residential mortgages has been negatively impacted by the generally unforeseen magnitude and rapidity in the collapse of housing prices.

Freddie Mac and Fannie Mae Had a Mandated Duty to Make Housing Affordable

Before I conclude, I just want to take a moment to recall the public mission of the GSEs. As everyone is aware, Freddie Mac is a shareholder-owned corporation, chartered for the public purpose of supporting America's mortgage finance markets, and operating under government mandates. We had obligations to Congress and to the public to promote our chartered purposes of increasing affordability, liquidity and stability in housing finance, which included some very specific low-income housing goals. We also had obligations to our regulator to pursue our goals in a manner that was prudent and reasonable. And, at the same time, we had fiduciary obligations to our shareholders that were the same as any other publicly traded company. Freddie Mac always worked hard to balance these multiple obligations, and for decades the company was effective.

There is much to be said about the successes of the GSE model, and those successes should not be overlooked because of the current crises. As Congress looks to the future of residential housing finance, the GSEs can and should play an important role.

> "Wall Street bankers ... [and their cronies in Washington] have systematically eviscerated the muscle and bones from the regulatory bodies charged with protecting us from banks' self-destructive greed."

Deregulation Is to Blame for the Financial Crisis

Shah Gilani

A former stock trader and financial services manager, Shah Gilani is currently a contributing editor at Money Morning, a daily news website for investors. In the following viewpoint, Gilani blames financial deregulation for the current economic crisis. According to Gilani, the banking industry systematically eroded strong regulations over time by winning influence in Congress and placing bankers into key government positions. Since the 1980s, these loyal bank cronies oversaw the dismantling of the Glass-Steagall Act that had separated banks by their functions (investment, commercial, etc.) and thus allowed commercial banks to begin trading in risky securities and derivatives, Gilani claims. In addition to new laws that lowered the amount

Shah Gilani, "How Deregulation Eviscerated the Banking Sector Safety Net and Spawned the U.S. Financial Crisis," moneymorning.com, January 13, 2009. Reprinted by permission.

of capital banks needed to keep in the Federal Reserve to back risky ventures, the overturning of Glass-Steagall paved the way for the subprime mortgage craze that made the banks millions on loans they no longer needed to personally secure, Gilani asserts. In his opinion, such precarious trading left banks insolvent when the housing market crashed.

As you read, consider the following questions:

1. As Gilani argues, what impact did the Garn-St. Germain Depository Institutions Act have on savings institutions' investments in real estate?

2. As Gilani reports, which chairperson of the US Commodity Futures Trading Commission oversaw the deregulation of bank swaps and derivatives trading?

3. In what year did the Securities and Exchange Commission rule that investment banks could determine their own net capital worth, according to Gilani?

No one person is responsible for the credit crisis, the failure of investment banks, the insolvency of commercial banks worldwide, the implosion of the world's stock markets, or for leading us to the precipice of another great depression.

The truth is there were many.

Fundamental and pragmatic banking regulations, which arose from the devastating financial collapses of the Great Depression, for decades strengthened U.S. banks and capital markets, making them the twin engines of American growth and the envy of the world.

The systematic dismantling of those same regulations by greedy bankers began in earnest in 1980, peaked in 1999, and finally climaxed with an insane Securities and Exchange Commission [SEC] ruling in April 2004, a final decision that paved the way for the implosion of everything regulation was designed to protect.

Just how did we get here?

Wall Street bankers, their exorbitantly well-paid lobbying army of former congressmen and former regulators, their greatly contributed-to sitting legislators and, most egregiously, the self-righteous and still mega-rich "former" Street executives have systematically eviscerated the muscle and bones from the regulatory bodies charged with protecting us from banks' self-destructive greed. An inordinately powerful group of executive insiders from the once-deeply respected House of Goldman Sachs (GS) have served as U.S. Treasury secretaries and in innumerable other administrative capacities.

Reform That Aids Bankers

The Depository Institutions Deregulation and Monetary Control Act of 1980, signed into law by President Jimmy Carter, was the first major reform of the U.S. banking system since the Great Depression.

While touted as a boon to consumers, the law was actually a gold mine for bankers. Among other requirements and banker "gifts" the 1980 Act's provisions:

- Lowered the mandatory reserve requirements banks keep in non-interest bearing accounts at U.S. Federal Reserve [Fed] banks.

- Established a five-member committee, the Depository Institutions Deregulation Committee, to phase out federal interest rate ceilings on deposit accounts over a six-year period.

- Increased Federal Deposit Insurance Corp. (FDIC) coverage from $40,000 to $100,000.

- Allowed depository institutions, including savings and loans and other thrift institutions, access to the Federal Reserve Discount Window for credit advances.

- And preempted state usury laws that limited the rates
lenders could charge on residential mortgage loans.

In 1980, in a virtual landslide, Ronald Reagan was elected
[president] and grabbed the conservative mantle. A year later,
the shock troops of the heralded Reagan Revolution launched
their attack and embarked on a massive, systematic deregulatory campaign. President Reagan's first Treasury secretary,
former Merrill Lynch & Co. [financial institution] Chief Executive Officer Donald T. Regan, became chairman of the Depository Institutions Deregulation Committee.

In a burst of deregulatory bravado in 1982, Treasury Secretary Regan ushered through the Garn-St. Germain Depository Institutions Act. Key provisions of the Act ultimately coa-
lesced with Treasury Secretary Regan's protection of the
lucrative "brokered deposits" business, in which Merrill was a
major player, and paved the way for the future collapse of the
savings and loan [S&L] industry.

Some of the provisions in that 1982 Act would later be
blamed for thousands of bank failures. The provisions permitted the following:

- Allowed savings and loans to make commercial, corporate, business or agricultural loans of up to 10% of
their assets.

- Authorized a capital assistance program—the "Net
Worth Certificate Program"—for dangerously undercapitalized banks, under which the Federal Savings and
Loan Insurance Corp. (FSLIC) and the FDIC would
purchase capital instruments called "Net Worth Certificates" from savings institutions with net worth/asset
ratios of less than 3.0%, and would theoretically later
redeem the certificates as these shaky banks regained
financial health.

- And, most frighteningly, raised the allowable ceiling on
direct investments by savings institutions in nonresi-
dential real estate from 20% to 40% of assets.

The history of S&L greed and fraud—which resulted from brokered deposits and deregulation—wasn't forgotten by legislators. But it was steamrolled by bankers pursuing an even greater unshackling of the regulations that constrained their ambitions.

Overturning Glass-Steagall

The ultimate prize was to be the undoing of the Glass-Steagall Act of 1933. Glass-Steagall, officially known as the Banking Act of 1933, mandated the separation of banks according to the types of business they conducted. Investment banks, whose securities-related activities resulted in relatively large risks, were to be separate from commercial banks, whose depositors needed greater protection. The Act created deposit insurance and the government wasn't about to allow taxpayer-backed insurance of commercial bank deposits to be exposed to securities-related risks. It was a prudent and sensible separation. Bankers tried for years to undermine and overturn Glass-Steagall, but it took time.

In 1987, Alan Greenspan replaced Paul A. Volcker—the stalwart Federal Reserve Board chairman, national inflation-fighting hero and active proponent of Glass-Steagall (and now economic confidant of President-elect [Barack] Obama).

In its twilight days, the Reagan administration was determined to further fertilize the seeds of deregulation and Greenspan's Ayn Rand[1]-inspired "objectivist," free market philosophies would be the perfect embodiment of the deregulatory movement.

Securitization Enters the Scene

A year later—in 1988—two very quiet revolutions sprouted that would ultimately hand bankers twin throttles to rain terror on us all.

---

1. A twentieth-century writer and philosopher, Ayn Rand's "objectivism" proposed a complete separation of government and economics.

That year, the Basel Accord [Basel I] established international risk-based capital requirements for deposit-taking commercial banks. In a by-product of the calculations of what constituted mortgage-related risk (by nature of the loans' long maturities and illiquidity) lenders should be expected to set aside substantial reserves; however, marketable securities that could theoretically be sold easily would not require significant reserves.

To obviate the need for such reserves, and to free up the money for more productive pursuits, banks made a wholesale shift from originating and holding mortgages to packaging them and holding mortgage assets in a now-securitized form. Not inconsequentially, this would lead to a disconnect between asset-quality considerations and asset-liquidity considerations.

Meanwhile, over at the U.S. Commodity Futures Trading Commission (CFTC), the appointment of free market disciple Wendy Gramm, wife of U.S. Sen. Phil Gramm, R-Tex., as chairperson, would result in her successful 1989 and 1993 exemption of swaps and derivatives from all regulation.

These actions would not be inconsequential in the aforementioned reign of terror that was still to come.

In 1993, with her agenda accomplished, Wendy Gramm resigned from her CFTC post to take a seat on the Enron Corp. board as a member of its audit committee. We all know what happened there. Enron's fraud and implosion became the poster child for deregulation run amok and ultimately helped spawn Sarbanes-Oxley legislation [designed to increase accurate financial reporting], which has its own issues.

The constant flow of money to lobbyists and into legislators' campaign coffers was paying off for the banking interests. The Fed, under Chairman Greenspan, was methodically deconstructing the foundation of Glass-Steagall. The final breaching of the wall occurred in 1998, when Citibank was bought by Travelers. The deal married Citibank, a commercial bank, with Travelers' Salomon Smith Barney invest-ment bank and the Travelers insurance business.

There was only one problem: The deal was clearly illegal in light of Glass-Steagall and the Bank Holding Company [BHC] Act of 1956 [which restricted bank involvement in non-banking businesses]. However, a legal loophole in the 1956 BHC Act gave the new Citicorp a five-year window to change the landscape, or the deal would have to be unwound. If aggressively flouting existing laws to pursue a personal agenda isn't a perfect example of bankers' hubris and greed, then maybe I've just got it all wrong.

Phil Gramm—the fire-breathing, free-marketer Texas sena-tor, and chairman of the U.S. Senate Committee on Banking, Housing and Urban Affairs—rode to the rescue, propelled by a sea of more than $300 million in lobbying and campaign contributions. In 1999, in the ultimate proof that money is power, U.S. President Bill Clinton signed into law the Gramm-Leach-Bliley [Act, also known as the] Financial Services Mod-ernization Act, at once doing away with Glass-Steagall and the 1956 BHC Act, and crowning Citigroup Inc. as the new "King of the Hill."

Opening the Subprime Flood Gates

From his position of power, Sen. Gramm consistently lever-aged his PhD in economics and free market ideology to es-pouse the virtues of subprime lending, where he famously once stated: "I look at subprime lending and I see the Ameri-can dream in action."

If helping struggling borrowers pursue their homeowner-ship dreams was such a noble cause, it might have been in-cumbent upon the senator to not block legislation advocating the curtailment of predatory lending practices. From 1989 through 2002, federal records show that Sen. Gramm was the top recipient of contributions from commercial banks and among the top five recipients of campaign contributions from Wall Street.

Since moving on from the Senate in 2002 to mega-universal Swiss banking giant UBS AG (UBS), where he serves as an investment banker and lobbyist, Gramm makes no apologies. "The markets have worked better than you might have thought," he has been quoted as saying. "There is this idea afloat that if you had more regulation you would have fewer mistakes. I don't see any evidence in our history or anybody else's to substantiate that."

Letting Banks Determine Their Own Health

On April 28, 2004, in a fitting and perhaps flagrant final act of eviscerating prudent regulation, the SEC ruled that investment banks may essentially determine their own net capital. The insanity of that allowance is only surpassed by the fact that the SEC allowed the change because it was simultaneously demanding greater scrutiny of the books and records of what were the holding companies of investment banks and all their affiliates.

The tragedy is that the SEC never used its new powers to examine the banks. The idea was that Consolidated Supervised Entities (CSEs) could use internal models to determine risk and compliance with net capital requirements. In reality, what the investment banks did was essentially recast hybrid capital instruments, subordinated debt, deferred tax returns and securities with no ready market into "healthy" capital assets against which they reduced reserve requirements for net capital calculations and increased their leverage [operating income divided by net income] to as much as 30:1.

When the meltdown came the leverage and concentration of bad assets quickly resulted in the shotgun marriage of insolvent Bear Stearns to JPMorgan Chase & Co. (JPM), the bankruptcy of Lehman Brothers Holdings (LEHMQ), the sale of Merrill Lynch to Bank of America Corp. (BAC), and the rushed acceptance of applications by Goldman and Morgan Stanley (MS) to convert to bank holding companies so they could feed at the taxpayer bailout trough and feast on the Fed's new smörgåsbord of liquidity handouts. There are no more CSEs (the SEC announced an end to that program in September [2008]). The old investment bank model is dead.

The Banks Are Writing Their Own Regulations

The motivation for bankers to undermine and inhibit prudent regulation is inherent in banker compensation incentives. The September 1993 *Journal of Financial Research* sums up the problem on compensation by concluding: "Firm characteristics that influence managerial compensation include leverage (as a measure of observable risk) market-to-book ratio of assets, size and shareholder return. Evidence suggests that bank holding companies may be exploiting the deposit insurance mechanism because leverage is a significant factor in our results for incentive-based components of compensation. Our results strongly support the view that fundamental shifts in business activities of bank holding companies have influenced their compensation strategies."

No one would tempt an alcoholic by putting one in charge of a liquor store and neither would anyone put a fox in charge of a henhouse. So why are greedy bankers being allowed to rewrite banking regulations to enrich themselves while leveraging taxpayers, destroying trillions of dollars of hard-earned savings and sinking us into a potential depression?

Until transparency sheds light on the backroom dealers and influence peddlers that aligned with Wall Street against Main Street, we will continue to be held hostage to the same greed and avarice that manifests itself in too many human beings who actually have the power to execute their personal agendas.

This is the story of how we got here. Where we are is actually even scarier than authorities are willing to admit.

> *"If there ever was an 'era of deregulation' in the financial world, it ended long ago. And the changes made then are for the most part noncontroversial today."*

Deregulation Is Not to Blame for the Financial Crisis

James L. Gattuso

In the following viewpoint, James L. Gattuso argues that supposed deregulation during the Republican presidency of George W. Bush cannot be blamed for the current financial crisis. According to Gattuso, the Bush era was not marked by deregulation; most reforms that eased rules on banking transactions occurred in the Democratic presidency of Bill Clinton. Gattuso maintains, though, that even these changes did not serve to aid the economic collapse in 2008. Clinton-era reforms helped banks spread risk, thus making them more stable, Gattuso claims. He attests that there never was a recent spate of deregulation and that all federal agencies tied to banking oversight have continued to perform their jobs without significant rule changes for more

James L. Gattuso, "Meltdowns and Myths: Did Deregulation Cause the Financial Crisis?" Heritage Foundation 2109, October 22, 2008. Reprinted by permission.

than a decade. James L. Gattuso is a research fellow in Regulatory Policy at the Thomas A. Roe Institute for Economic Policy Studies at the Heritage Foundation, a conservative public policy think tank.

As you read, consider the following questions:

1. In Gattuso's view, why was the repeal of the rule banning banks from operating in more than one state a wise decision?

2. Why does Gattuso believe that it is impossible to pin the blame for the financial crisis on legislation passed in 2000 that kept federal regulators from overseeing certain banking transactions such as credit default swaps and derivatives trading?

3. How does the author use the budgets of banking regulatory agencies to support his argument that deregulation did not occur in the last two decades?

E asy answers are seldom correct ones. That principle seems to be at work as the nation struggles to discover the causes of the financial crisis now rocking the economy. Looking for a simple and politically convenient villain, many politicians have blamed deregulation by the [George W.] Bush administration.

House Speaker Nancy Pelosi, for instance, stated last month [in September 2008] that "the Bush administration's eight long years of failed deregulation policies have resulted in our nation's largest bailout ever, leaving the American taxpayers on the hook potentially for billions of dollars." Similarly, presidential candidate Barack Obama asserted in the second presidential debate that "the biggest problem in this whole process was the deregulation of the financial system."

But there is one problem with this answer: Financial services were not deregulated during the Bush administration. If there ever was an "era of deregulation" in the financial world, it ended long ago. And the changes made then are for the most part noncontroversial today.

Regulations Are Still in Place

In a literal sense, financial services were never "deregulated," nor was there ever a serious attempt to do so. Few analysts have ever proposed the elimination of the regulatory structures in place to ensure the soundness and transparency of banks. Simply put, the job of bank examiner was never threatened.

More typically, of course, the word *deregulation* has been used as shorthand to describe the repeal or easing of particular rules. To the extent there was a heyday of such deregulation, it was in the 1970s and 1980s. It was at this time that economists—and consumer activists—began to question many long-standing restrictions on financial services.

The most important such restrictions were rules banning banks from operating in more than one state. Such rules were largely eliminated by 1994 through state and federal action. Few observers lament their passing today, and because regional and nationwide banks are far better able to balance risk, this "deregulation" has helped mitigate, rather than contribute to, the instability of the system.

Easing Rules to Prevent More Harm

The next major "deregulation" of financial services was the repeal of the Depression-era prohibition on banks engaging in the securities business. The ban was formally ended by the 1999 Gramm-Leach-Bliley Act [also known as the Financial Services Modernization Act], which followed a series of decisions by regulators easing its impact.

While not without controversy, the net effect of Gramm-Leach-Bliley has likely been to alleviate rather than further the current financial crisis.

In fact, President Bill Clinton—who signed the reform bill into law—defended the legislation in a recent interview, saying, "I don't see that signing that bill had anything to do with the current crisis. Indeed, one of the things that has helped stabilize the current situation as much as it has is the purchase of Merrill Lynch by Bank of America, which was much smoother than it would have been if I hadn't signed that bill."

In 2000, Congress also passed legislation that, among other things, clarified that certain kinds of financial instruments were not regulated by the Commodity Futures Trading Commission (CFTC). Among these were "credit default swaps," which have played a role in this year's meltdown. Whether this law constituted "deregulation" is not clear, since the prelegislation status of these instruments was uncertain. Nor is it a given that CFTC regulation of their trading would have avoided the financial crisis. In fact, many policy makers, including Clinton Treasury Secretary Robert Rubin, argued that their regulation would do more harm than good.

In the nine years since that legislation—including the eight years of the Bush presidency—Congress has enacted no further legislation easing burdens of the financial services industry.

Few Federal Rule Changes

But what of the regulatory agencies? Did they pursue a deregulatory agenda during the Bush administration? Again, the answer seems to be no.

In terms of rule making—the promulgation of specific rules by regulatory agencies—the Securities and Exchange Commission (SEC) is by far the most active among agencies in the financial realm. Based on data from the Government Accountability Office, the SEC completed 23 proceedings since the beginning of the Bush administration that resulted in a substantive and major change (defined as an economic effect of $100 million or more) in regulatory burdens. Of those, only eight—about a third—lessened burdens. Perhaps surprisingly, the Bush record in this regard is actually less deregula-

Risk Is Part of a Healthy Marketplace

People can only achieve bold successes when they take risks. The virtue of the market is that it allows individuals the freedom to risk their own money—or that of investors whom they can convince to fund them voluntarily—reaping the rewards if they succeed and bearing the losses if they fail. There is no reason to suppose that government bureaucrats would have designed better models of risk assessment. Indeed, two Fed [Federal Reserve] economists wrote a paper in 2005 claiming that there was no housing bubble!

Robert P. Murphy,
"Did Deregulated Derivatives Cause the Financial Crisis?"
Freeman, *March 2009.*

tory than that of the Clinton administration, which during its second term lessened burdens in nine out of 20 such rule making proceedings.

Other financial agencies have been far less active in making formal rule changes. The Federal Reserve [Fed] reports five major rule makings in the database since 1996—four of which were deregulatory. The only rule change reported by the Federal Deposit Insurance Corporation and the [Office of the] Comptroller of the Currency is the 1997 adoption of new capital reserve standards, an action with mixed consequences.

Of course, much of the work of regulators takes place in day-to-day activities rather than in formal rule making activities. For that reason, it is also helpful to look at the budgets of regulators.

These also show little sign of reduced regulatory activity during the Bush years. The total budget of federal finance and banking regulators (excluding the SEC) increased from approximately $2 billion in FY [fiscal year] 2000 to almost $2.3 billion in FY 2008 in constant 2000 dollars. The SEC's budget during the same time period jumped from $357 million in 2000 to a whopping $629 million in 2008. During the same time period, total staffing at these agencies remained steady, at close to 16,000.

There Never Was an Ideal Era of Regulation

In the wake of the financial crisis gripping the nation, it is tempting to blame "deregulation" for triggering the problem. After all, if the meltdown were caused by the ill-advised elimination of necessary rules, the answer would be easy: Restore those rules.

But that story line is simply not true. Not only was there little deregulation of financial services during the Bush years, but most of the regulatory reforms achieved in earlier years mitigated, rather than contributed to, the crisis.

This, of course, does not mean that no regulatory changes should be considered. In the wake of the current crisis, debate over the scope and method of regulation in financial markets is inevitable and, in fact, necessary. But this cannot be a debate over returning to a regulatory Nirvana that never existed. Any new regulatory system would be just that—complete with all the uncertainty and prospects for unintended consequences that define such a system. Policy makers must not pretend otherwise.

| "There is, in short, plenty of blame to go around."

Many Share the Blame for the Financial Crisis

Mortimer B. Zuckerman

Mortimer B. Zuckerman is the editor in chief of U.S. News & World Report. *In the viewpoint that follows, Zuckerman claims that it is impossible and unjust to pin the blame for the current financial crisis on one source. Instead, he believes most of America shares the responsibility for the disaster—politicians who encouraged banks to make risky loans to home buyers with poor credit, average Americans who took out mortgages and other credit loans they could not afford, and banks that gorged on the glut of non-asset-backed securities that sprang from these loan deals. Zuckerman contends that understanding the various origins of the problem will better prepare the public and law-makers to fairly judge the coming proposals for rebuilding the economy.*

Mortimer B. Zuckerman, "Who to Blame for the Financial Crisis," *U.S. News & World Report*, January 29, 2010. Reprinted by permission.

As you read, consider the following questions:

1. What faults does Zuckerman lay at the feet of the Bush and Obama administrations in relation to the crisis?

2. According to Zuckerman, how did Fannie Mae and Freddie Mac escape tighter regulations that might have restricted their acceptance of so many risky mortgages?

3. What percentage of interest-only or negative-amortization loans were packaged into securities by banks and sold worldwide, as Zuckerman reports?

Class warfare, American style, is being waged between Main Street and Wall Street. With President [Barack] Obama and Democrats in Congress turning up the populist heat against Wall Street, the financial community is losing. Its back is up against the wall. But the administration is also getting its share of the public's rage, as we saw in the devastating defeat of the Democratic candidate [Martha Coakley] in the Massachusetts Senate race [January 2010].

Who's really to blame?

It's easy to see why Main Street America is seething at Wall Street for its role in our present afflictions. We endure an unconscionable national unemployment rate that shows little sign of easing. There's justifiable anxiety among the employed or partly employed that they will be the next to lose their jobs. Millions fear that the devaluation of their home equity, 401(k)s, and other financial assets means that we are not just being shaken by a little bump but have fallen into an abyss, a free fall that will play havoc with plans for retirement and the ability to provide for the education of the next generation.

All this heightens Main Street's sense of victimization. Americans see a financial world that was saved by taxpayers footing the bill for an unprecedented rescue, after which bankers walked away not only without a scratch but with executives' pockets abulge with bonuses out of all proportion to the way most Americans live and work.

The American Public Is Complicit in the Financial Crisis

There's plenty of fuel here for the most raw form of populism—and the president and the Democratic-controlled Congress are ready to exploit it. President Obama's response within two days of the Massachusetts election was to announce he would limit dramatically the activities of banks and increase their costs and taxes—all in the context that they are the principal perpetrators of the Great Recession.

But that's both opportunistic and simplistic. Victory always has a thousand fathers; defeat is always an orphan. A realistic examination of the history suggests that a fairer verdict is that our catastrophe has any number of fathers: homeowners as well as mortgage lenders; borrowers and consumers as well as bankers; political leaders of both parties as well as corporations' chief executives; not just a lamentably dozy Securities and Exchange Commission but reckless government-supported mortgage agencies (Freddie Mac and Fannie Mae); the august Federal Reserve Bank; and the commercial rating agencies. The American public, by default, was complicit. For at least a generation, U.S. consumers overspent and undersaved, while simultaneously accumulating large personal debts. They purchased homes they couldn't pay for with mortgages they couldn't afford.

Politicians Helped Create the Housing Bubble

And then there are the administrations of George W. Bush and Barack Obama. The Bush years saw unsustainable budget deficits and massive trade deficits, all requiring huge funding. Bush lowered taxes and waged wars without cutting spending or raising revenues. The Obama administration understandably loses no chance to remind us of these eight reckless years. But while it was swift in its first year to do more to extinguish the flames in the basement, the current administration failed in rebuilding the economy to concentrate on jobs, jobs and to focus on energizing the economy. It allowed Congress to give a job-stimulus program a bad name by distorting where the money would go (and go far too slowly).

Politicians in both parties share blame for long pressuring the banks and mortgage companies to facilitate homeowner-ship for minorities and people who would have difficulty paying. By 2007, the regulations of the Department of Housing and Urban Development stipulated that 55 percent of the loans that Fannie Mae [Federal National Mortgage Association] and Freddie Mac [Federal Home Loan Mortgage Corporation] made had to go to borrowers at or below the median income level. And nearly half of these loans had to be to low-income borrowers. The Democratic chairman of the House Financial Services Committee, Rep. Barney Frank, seems to have forgotten his assertion that he was willing to "roll the dice" on subsidized housing, denying there was any cause for concern. For the better part of a decade, Fannie and Freddie were bringing on risky mortgages that loaded the dice heavily against the taxpayer. They had a huge advantage in capital costs because of an implicit government guarantee. This enabled them to ramp up mortgage lending programs to less creditworthy borrowers at high margins and with exorbitant fees. The low-cost capital the banks were able to accumulate through low-cost federal funds and foreign oil revenues found its way into the U.S. residential real estate market, fostering the housing bubble.

U.S. home prices grew by an average of 3 percent per year from 1945 to 2001. During the next five years, they rose at an estimated 16 percent annually. That includes homes that took on mortgages to extract equity, helping to reduce the equity content in U.S. housing from nearly 70 percent in 1965 to 43 percent in 2007.

At the same time, Freddie and Fannie wriggled out of tighter regulation by donating thousands of dollars to political action committees.

Toxic Loans Go Bad

The disastrous subprime market was thus the creature not so much of Wall Street as of our political leaders, who created the subprime market by pressing banks to make riskier loans and then virtually compelling Fannie and Freddie to liquefy these toxic assets by putting more and more of them on their own balance sheets. Fannie and Freddie had been buying risky loans since 1993 to meet the "affordable housing" requirements established by Congress. No one in successive administrations effectively monitored the consequences, especially the workings of the 1977 Community Reinvestment Act, which was designed to make loans available in poorer communities. Obsessed by this political objective, Democrats would not support regulations suggested by the Republicans in the Senate Committee [on Banking, Housing and Urban Affairs] in 2005 that would have established more auditing and oversight.

The result? At the end of 2008, these two agencies held or guaranteed about 10 million subprime and Alt-A mortgages [Alternative A-paper loans, issued to borrowers with poor credit or incomplete documentation] through mortgage-backed securities. These hazardous loans had a principal balance of $1.6 trillion. These are the loans that began to default at unprecedented rates in 2008 and 2009 and forced the government to take control of Fannie and Freddie, which then continued to buy dicey mortgages to minimize the housing crisis.

More troubling, Peter Wallison's report in the *Wall Street Journal* on research by Edward Pinto, a former chief credit officer at Fannie Mae, says that "from the time Fannie and Freddie began buying risky loans . . . they routinely misrepresented the mortgages . . . as prime when they had characteristics that made them clearly subprime or Alt-A." According to Wallison, "Of the 26 million subprime and Alt-A loans outstanding in 2008, 10 million were held or guaranteed by Fannie and Freddie, 5.2 million by other government agencies, and 1.4 million were still on the books of the four largest U.S. banks." And 7.7 million subprime and Alt-A housing loans were in mortgage pools supporting mortgage-backed securities issued by Wall Street banks.

Where were the rating agencies when this house of cards was being built? Most of the loans were rated AAA. But what did that mean?

The raters went merrily along assuming that any losses incurred from defaults would be within the historical range. But the assumptions were false, in part because of irrational exuberance and in part because of the mislabeling of defaults and actual losses after foreclosures exceeded all prior experience. Everybody was incurring unprecedented losses and deficits, but the rating agencies and regulators seemed to have lost touch with reality.

Bundling and Selling Off Loan Securities

In the meantime, while the party was on, some 75 percent of the interest-only or negative-amortization loans [loans on which monthly payments were less than the monthly interest charge] that didn't require near-term principal payments were packaged into securities. The banks sold these and other complex financial products as securities worldwide to monetize a lending binge of consumer loans of all flavors: mortgages, home equity lines, credit cards, auto loans, student loans, and commercial real estate. Many mortgages were too large in relation to the real value of the homes, and some were taken out to support lifestyles by drawing down the equity in the homes. When the housing bubble burst and homeowners could no longer service the mortgages, the default rate soared to levels never before experienced or contemplated—way beyond the 1 percent to 2 percent during good times or even the 6 percent to 7 percent during recessions, to levels of nearly 10 percent for fixed rate mortgages, more than 25 percent for subprime adjustable rate mortgages, and almost 60 percent for option adjustable rate mortgages.

Not surprisingly, investors lost confidence in the ratings; they fled the market for mortgage-backed securities and ultimately withdrew entirely from all asset-backed securities. The result was to destroy the capital of private mortgage lenders like Countrywide, Washington Mutual, and Golden West, as well as Wall Street firms such as Bear Stearns, Merrill Lynch, and Lehman Brothers, not to mention Fannie and Freddie.

Their financial assets could no longer be sold, except at seriously discounted prices. This, in turn, undermined the confidence, stability, and even the solvency of some of the world's largest financial institutions. A freeze-up followed in interbank lending as one crisis fed into another, putting many major banks under water. The global credit markets ground to a halt. Interest rates soared and loan availability plummeted, resulting in the implosion of the world's asset markets, including global equity markets. The end result was the Great Recession, which plagues us to this day.

There is, in short, plenty of blame to go around, and it's important to understand the origins of the crisis to judge the fairness and efficacy of the restrictions and taxes that the Obama administration now proposes for the banks.

Periodical and Internet Sources Bibliography

The following articles have been selected to supplement the diverse views presented in this chapter.

Christian Science Monitor	"Financial Reform on Wall Street After the Bailouts: The Wrong Focus," April 14, 2010.
Veronique de Rugy	"We Didn't Deregulate," *National Review Online*, April 5, 2010. www.nationalreview.com.
Niall Ferguson	"Wall Street's New Gilded Age," *Newsweek*, September 11, 2009.
Jeffrey Friedman	"Bank Pay and the Financial Crisis," *Wall Street Journal*, September 28, 2009.
Stephen Gandel	"Why Your Bank Is Broke," *Time*, January 31, 2009.
Paul Krugman	"Rewarding Bad Actors," *New York Times*, August 2, 2009.
Mark Levinson	"The Economic Collapse," *Dissent*, Winter 2009.
Katherine Mangu-Ward	"Is Deregulation to Blame?" *Reason*, January 2009.
Allan H. Meltzer	"Reflections on the Financial Crisis," *Cato Journal*, Winter 2009.
Robert J. Shiller	"Mom, Apple Pie and Mortgages," *New York Times*, March 6, 2010.
Jacob Weisberg	"What Caused the Great Recession?" *Newsweek*, January 9, 2010.

OPPOSING
VIEWPOINTS®
SERIES

Does Wall Street Need Financial Reform?

Chapter Preface

When the housing bubble burst in 2008, the resulting financial crisis left many looking for a scapegoat. The obvious target was Wall Street banking institutions—those same businesses that authorized subprime mortgages and traded them as securities through subsidiary companies to buyers worldwide. Politicians were quick to point fingers at big banks, suggesting that money-hungry Wall Street had lost touch with the average workers living on Main Street.

In his bid for the presidency in 2008, Republican candidate and US senator from Arizona John McCain told a crowd in Tampa, Florida, "This foundation of our economy, the American worker, is strong but it has been put at risk by the greed and mismanagement of Wall Street and Washington." McCain claimed that government abetted the disaster by lacking a clear regulatory system and by funding government-sponsored enterprises such as Fannie Mae (the Federal National Mortgage Association) and Freddie Mac (the Federal Home Loan Mortgage Corporation) that inflated the subprime loan market. McCain's Democratic opponent, Senator Barack Obama of Illinois, criticized government deregulation in a speech delivered in New York in March 2008 but only insofar as legislators "failed to guard against practices that all too often rewarded financial manipulation instead of productivity and sound business practices." Later in an April 2010 speech, Obama, now president, stated more pointedly, "Some on Wall Street forgot that behind every dollar traded or leveraged, there is a family looking to buy a house, pay for an education, open a business, or save for retirement."

The political rhetoric was clear: Wall Street was unconcerned with Main Street, and it was up to average Americans to reclaim financial security and national prosperity from greedy banks. These sentiments spread throughout the country and were echoed by many analysts and pundits. Peter

Fenn, a media firm chief executive officer, wrote an April 28, 2010, blog post that warned readers how unhealthy it is for the biggest banks in the United States to have assets worth almost two-thirds of the nation's gross domestic product. Calling for immediate congressional action, Fenn asserted, "Let's keep the pressure on and stop the bank behemoths from becoming even bigger and swallowing all of us."

Meanwhile, some critics argued that Wall Street was merely a whipping boy for those who did not want to admit their complicity in the financial crisis. CNN contributor David Frum wrote in an April 26, 2010, column that much of the blame rested with average Americans who took on risky mortgages and expanded their debts beyond their means. Though Frum believes Americans incurred a lot of debt because incomes are not rising fast enough to meet expenses, he maintains the crash resulted from an untenable economy in which consumer debt ballooned to 96 percent of the gross domestic product. Other observers such as financial analyst Markos Kaminis also chastened consumers while being more lenient on Wall Street's supposed wrongdoings. Writing for the Seeking Alpha website on September 29, 2008, Kaminis stated, "Wall Street did nothing more than create financial securities, specifically secondary markets in asset-backed securities, that allowed Americans to live the American dream. They created securities, they bought them and sold them, held them for investment and traded them for fee. That's all they did. Meanwhile, as a result, the everyday Joe was able to own a home and a new car too." Kaminis insists that American society—which, he argues, promotes easy living and an attitude of entitlement—failed to protect itself against banking misdeeds as well as its own acquisitive vices.

In the following chapter, reporters, economists, and bankers address the issue of blame and offer reasons why big banking institutions should or should not be reformed as a result of the financial crisis.

> *"It is time for change and the place to start is in the corporate boardrooms of America."*

Wall Street Needs Reform

Carl C. Icahn

Carl C. Icahn is the chairman of Icahn Enterprises, a holding company with shares in the real estate, automotive, railway, and other industries. In the viewpoint that follows, Icahn argues that while government bailouts may stabilize the failed economic system, only by reshaping corporate management can Congress ensure that another greed-driven financial catastrophe will not take place. Icahn claims that lawmakers should give more power to shareholders to rein in the risk-taking excesses of industry leaders. Icahn believes that in doing so, shareholders can keep executives from speculating with corporate money that does not belong to them.

As you read, consider the following questions:

1. What two federal-level laws would Icahn like Congress to enact to improve the influence of shareholders in the management of companies?

Carl C. Icahn, "The Economy Needs Corporate Governance Reform," *Wall Street Journal*, January 23, 2009. Reprinted by permission.

2. In Icahn's view, what "one simple provision" could Congress pass to give more power to shareholders at the state level?

3. What three things does Icahn say contributed to the "entirely preventable" financial meltdown?

In his inaugural address this week [in January 2009], President Barack Obama said "our economy is badly weakened, a consequence of greed and irresponsibility on the part of some," and due in part to "our collective failure to make hard choices."

He's offered few policy specifics other than saying we need to undertake massive new infrastructure and education programs. But he is right, there are a lot of hard choices we need to make. And one of them is the decision to fix the way public companies are managed.

Private enterprise forms the basis for our economy. It provides most of the jobs we enjoy and creates the wealth that raises living standards. New government spending can only do so much to repair the economy. Reshaping corporate management can do much more.

The Price of Doing Nothing

The problem with doing nothing is obvious. Faltering companies are now soaking up hundreds of billions of tax dollars, and they are not substantially changing their management structures as a price for taking this money.

How does it serve the economy when we subsidize managements that got their companies into trouble? Where is the accountability? More importantly, where are the results?

The economy continues to sink, jobs are being lost, the markets continue on a downward course. Changes are needed and can come if Congress insists on reforms that make corporate boards and managers more accountable to stakeholders.

More Devastating than a Terrorist Attack

What we don't know will hurt us, and quite possibly on a more devastating scale than any al Qaeda [terrorist group] attack. Americans must be told the full story of how Wall Street gamed and inflated the housing bubble, made out like bandits, and then left millions of households in ruin. Without that reckoning, there will be no public clamor for serious reform of a financial system that was as cunningly breached as airline security at the Amsterdam airport [where, in December 2009, an al Qaeda operative successfully boarded an airliner headed for Detroit].

Frank Rich,
"The Other Plot to Wreck America,"
New York Times, *January 10, 2010.*

What Congress Must Do

First, Congress needs to pass legislation giving shareholders enhanced rights to elect new boards, submit resolutions for stockholder votes, and have far more input on executive compensation and other issues. As companion to these reforms, Congress needs to pass legislation that prevents managers from making it more difficult for shareholders to exercise their ownership rights.

Managers often come up with creative ways to perpetuate their reigns of error. These include myriad takeover obstacles like poison pills [building in negative consequences to any attempt to take over a company], bylaw provisions [giving boards of directors the right, without consulting stockholders, to issue preferred stock at their discretion], and other devices that thwart shareholder efforts to hold managers accountable.

If Congress is reluctant to make wholesale changes at the federal level, it can enact one simple provision that would allow many of the needed changes to take place on the state level: It can give shareholders the right to vote to move a company's legal jurisdiction to a more shareholder-friendly state such as North Dakota. Currently that decision is in the hands of company boards.

It is not reasonable to expect managers with failing track records to improve their performance on their own. They will only improve if they are placed under greater pressure by shareholders empowered to exert more influence on management decisions. Nothing will do more to improve our economy than corporate governance changes.

Private Industry Is the Backbone of America's Financial Strength

What we need are measures that let the capitalist system produce jobs and economic activity, with minimal but effective government oversight. Government spending is an important catalyst to economic gains, but we need to focus on improving the way private companies are managed so private capital can flow into them.

Our private sector is the greatest wealth creation machine ever devised, far outperforming any other economic model. Still, major improvements could do a lot to mitigate what Mr. Obama calls "the sapping of confidence across our land."

Lax and ineffective boards, self-serving managements, and failed short-term strategies all contributed to the entirely preventable financial meltdown. It is time for battered shareholders to fight back.

Mr. Obama was right when he said that "it has been the risk-takers, the doers, the makers of things . . . who have carried us up the long, rugged path towards prosperity and freedom."

I hope this means that the day of reckoning has come for those executives who simply feed at public and private troughs, putting little or no capital of their own at risk, and who produce little of value for the national economy.

It is time for change and the place to start is in the corporate boardrooms of America.

| "The wizards of Wall Street may have concocted exotic ways to make money by betting on the fortunes of the real-estate market, but it was the politicans who first destabilized that market."

Government Fiscal Policy Needs Reform Before Instituting Wall Street Reform

Mona Charen

In the following viewpoint, Mona Charen explains the Democrats' justification for the financial crisis of 2008, which primarily blames Wall Street bankers for manipulating markets behind closed doors. Charen disagrees with the mostly Democratic call for Wall Street reform, which would require more transparency of Wall Street borrowing practices. While Charen agrees that Wall Street "may deserve flaying," more important, Charen insists, is reforming government fiscal policy. While Wall Street may be to blame in part, Charen points out that the federal budget deficit stands at $1.5 trillion, something that should be looked into first, before blaming Wall Street trades between consenting parties. Mona Charen is a nationally syndicated columnist.

Mona Charen, "Who's More Irresponsible, Wall Street or State Governments?" *National Review*, April 30, 2010. www.nationalreview.com. Reproduced by permission.

As you read, consider the following questions:

1. What, according to Charen, is the Democrats' narrative about the financial crisis of 2008?

2. What is the problem with the Dodd bill, according to the author of the viewpoint?

3. How much does the average state now owe, according to the viewpoint?

The Democrats' narrative about the financial crisis of 2008 (and their justification for financial reform) goes like this: Investment bankers, typified by Goldman Sachs, manipulated markets, bamboozled investors, and in their greed managed to bring the entire economy to its knees. The solution is more strenuous government regulation, but Republicans, who are beholden to Wall Street, are blocking reform.

The Democrats' Justification for Financial Reform

The Democrats excel at presenting legislative tableaux with predigested morals: Stern Democratic lawmaker grills slippery Wall Street executive; Democrats for the people, Republicans for the fat cats.

Do people really buy this anymore? Everyone I know who works on Wall Street is a Democrat. Anecdotes are not evidence, but consider this: According to the Center for Responsive Politics, Democrats received $11.3 million in contributions from hedge funds in 2008. Republicans got $5.9 million. Some critics of the Dodd bill note that it would give broad discretion to the FDIC [Federal Deposit Insurance Corporation] and a new regulator to decide which firms would be bailed out and which would not. That isn't so much preventing another crisis as institutionalizing "too big to fail." The moral hazard problem—i.e. encouraging risky practices with the implicit or explicit promise of a bailout—remains.

Furthermore, the Dodd bill—and the Democrats' narrative—completely omits the role of government in the financial debacle. Neither Fannie Mae nor Freddie Mac is mentioned in the legislation. But the incentives created by government, specifically the sustained push through law and regulation to provide mortgages to more and more uncreditworthy borrowers, created the conditions for the housing bubble and for its eventual crash. The wizards of Wall Street may have concocted exotic ways to make money by betting on the fortunes of the real-estate market, but it was the politicians who first destabilized that market.

Does Wall Street Need Reform?

Let's stipulate that the masters of the universe on Wall Street may deserve flaying, and sensible reform requiring more transparency and limiting leverage is well and good. But when the federal budget deficit stands at $1.5 trillion, the spectacle of congressmen and senators waxing indignant about the irresponsibility of others is a bit much.

Leaders have a responsibility to be prudent with the taxpayers' money. At least Wall Street trades are between consenting parties. But when politicians gamble with taxpayer money, it's different. We don't willingly sign on to these bets. Yet by their profligacy, elected officials are placing our financial futures at severe risk.

Nicole Gelinas, writing in *City Journal,* sketches what may be the next crash to rock our world. It's another investment, like housing, that people assume cannot fail—municipal bonds. They are risk free, investors have long been assured, because the cities and states that issue them would do anything to avoid default. Besides, "they . . . have a captive source of endless funds. . . . State and local governments . . . can always tax their residents and businesses to pay the bills."

Between 2000 and 2008, states were rolling in cash, pulling in tax revenues that outpaced inflation by 15 percent. But instead of using this windfall to reduce their debts, states continued to spend freely, particularly on expensive union contracts, education, and Medicaid. When the recession began, Gelinas notes, "state and local officials should have realized that hard fiscal times were coming and begun cutting back. . . . Instead they kept on spending, and borrowed to do it." States are now deeply in debt. The most extreme cases—California, New York, and New Jersey—are well known. But the average state now owes 2.1 percent of its residents' annual income.

The Problem with Government Stimulus

The 2009 stimulus bill only exacerbated the problem by pumping $200 billion in "reality-distorting funds" into state and municipal coffers, delaying the reckoning and permitting states to continue their reckless spending.

What will happen when states can no longer sustain the public-employee pensions and health benefits, the Medicaid payments, and the education spending? Gelinas offers a glimpse of a possible future in the case of Vallejo, Calif. The city declared bankruptcy in 2008 to escape from crippling union contracts. Vallejo was successful, but in the process, it delayed payments on its bonds for three years. Other bondholders might not be so lucky. It's not hard, Gelinas writes "to imagine some future mayor convincing a bankruptcy judge that it's only fair for bondholders, along with union members, to take big cuts in a restructuring."

When Democrats preen that they are fighting for the average guy, ask this: When they vastly overspend, what happens to the ordinary person who dutifully pays his taxes and prudently invests in "safe" municipal bonds?

"No entity or instrument should be untouched by some form of regulation."

Government Should Revamp the Regulation System

Jesse Eisinger

In the following viewpoint, Jesse Eisinger writes that the financial crisis that collapsed markets in 2008 provides Congress with an opportunity to increase regulation on banking practices. According to Eisinger, old regulations did not have sufficient power to halt wild speculation, and regulators were too timid in applying what leverage they did have. Eisinger advocates that the oversight of banking be reduced to two agencies—one to monitor the stability of financial institutions and the other to safeguard investors. In this way, he hopes that big banks will always be on guard against overstepping their bounds for fear of incurring the penalties of shoddy business practices. Eisinger also hopes that the financial crisis will entice more whistleblowers and plaintiff lawyers to stand up to the huge financial industry to keep pressure on boardrooms to conform to the regulations. A former Wall Street Journal *market analyst, Jesse Eisinger now serves as the* Wall Street *editor at Portfolio.com.*

Jesse Eisinger, "First, Fire the Regulators," Portfolio.com, January 7, 2009. Reprinted with permission.

As you read, consider the following questions:

1. Why does Eisinger believe the time is right for Congress to finally pass meaningful Wall Street reform?

2. According to Eisinger, what should be done with the regulatory powers of the Federal Reserve?

3. Explain why the author thinks the "Twin Peaks" approach to regulation will create a beneficial good-cop, bad-cop system?

In the aftermath of the stock market crash of 1987, reformers moved to remake America's regulatory structure. Some experts proposed tinkering with the oversight agencies, merging the Securities and Exchange Commission [SEC] with the Commodity Futures Trading Commission [CFTC], for instance. Others recommended regulating derivatives, which were in their infancy. [Financial speculator and businessman] George Soros, not yet the bëte noire [bane] of right-wingers, took to the editorial page of the *Wall Street Journal* to warn that nobody was thinking big enough: "The longer markets function without supervision explicitly aimed at maintaining stability, the greater the danger of an accident like October 19, 1987."

Anyone remember the landmark 1987 Securities Act? It never materialized. And did anything happen in 1998, after Long-Term Capital Management nearly went under and a similar dance took place? Many of the same players strutted on the same stage, and Soros again predicted that without sweeping international regulatory reform, we risked "the breakdown of the gigantic circulatory system which goes under the name of global capitalism." Again, no '98 Securities Act—perhaps not surprising, given that what followed was a market recovery that we now know was a massive equity bubble.

A Crisis That Calls for Reform

In our current financial mess, hardly a day goes by without another hearing on the failures of the U.S. regulatory system or speech on regulatory affairs. In November [2008], Henry Waxman, chairman of the House Committee on Oversight and Government Reform, hauled five of the most influential hedge fund managers before the committee and extracted pronouncements from each of them—some less full-throated than others—that the markets, including hedge funds, needed more regulation. Once again, there was George Soros, as right as ever, leading the Regulatory Light Brigade.

This time, the calamity in the markets is more devastating than any of the previous crises since the Great Depression. Luckily, it's looking like history won't repeat itself. One of the enduring legacies of this economic collapse will be that the government finally had to embark on a wholesale financial re-thinking. Right now [January 2009], finding a way to end the crisis and reinvigorate the economy is the most pressing issue. But in a few months, after the [Barack] Obama administration settles in—assuming we aren't all eating cat food under a bridge—we are going to have the debate we need about how to rebuild the regulatory system.

The pressure to put off this debate will be enormous. The financial industry is bound to resist. But Wall Street is at its weakest point in decades: The new administration has to strike while the public temper is at its hottest.

"Investors have lost confidence in everything: the regulators, the system, the oversight of Congress, the fairness of our markets," says Arthur Levitt, a former SEC chairman. "How do you restore that?"

One hopeful sign is that President Obama has given the matter significant thought. In a campaign speech in March, he talked about regulating the derivatives markets and raising the capital standards for banks. If that speech becomes the template for reform, it's a promising start. It's also promising that

Gary Gensler was named co-head of Obama's search team for a new SEC leader. Gensler has been a prescient critic of excesses at [the government-sponsored mortgage market enterprises known as] Fannie Mae [Federal National Mortgage Association] and Freddie Mac [Federal Home Loan Mortgage Corporation] (which were not remotely the cause of the crisis but were inarguably pockets of systemic risk).

Failures of the Old Regulating Regime

First, regulators need to change their ninnyish attitudes. They have gone about their jobs in the past decade like hall monitors at the prom, deeply afraid of being ostracized. They need to bring some mettle to their roles. The challenge is to remake the system so that it's up to the task of preventing, or at least minimizing, the next global meltdown. Alter the structure all you want, but unless you have the right regulatory attitude, it'll be for naught.

This is not a moment to think small. First, we raze the SEC and the CFTC, along with most, if not all, of the federal banking and state insurance regulatory structure. We should strip the Federal Reserve of its responsibility for regulating banks; it's enough to oversee the economy. And just as everyone was trying to express how bumbling and irrelevant the SEC's enforcement approach has been, the agency provided perfect examples.

In mid-November [2008], headlines blared that the SEC had charged Mark Cuban, the billionaire owner of the Dallas Mavericks and a frequent blogger, with insider trading. Did he gain secret knowledge of the failure of AIG [American International Group] and sell his stake? Had he done something untoward with regard to Lehman Brothers [a financial firm that declared bankruptcy in 2008 as a result of the market crisis]? No. Four and a half years ago, Cuban sold stock in a company called Mamma.com based on inside information, according to the SEC, and thereby avoided $750,000 in losses.

Today, Copernic, Mamma.com's successor, sports a market value of less than $3 million. Cuban may well be guilty. But who cares? It's as if Homeland Security had a ceremony in 2008 to announce that it had erected a gold-plated bollard at ground zero. And come December, it became clear that the SEC had shockingly botched multiple chances to upend confessed Ponzi schemer [investment fraud operator] Bernie Madoff.

Before the economic crisis became acute, Treasury Secretary Hank [Henry] Paulson put forward his plan to remake the regulatory system. Like most of Paulson's initiatives, it was inadequately explained and poorly sold. And the motivation was exactly wrong, born of a fear of regulation that looks ridiculous today. It died on arrival, as it should have.

The Twin Peaks Approach

But surprisingly enough, given the dubious way it began, a Paulson-like framework is a good place to start. It was influenced by what is known in regulatory circles as the Twin Peaks approach, used in Australia and the Netherlands. The idea is to create two financial regulators that are given separate responsibilities not based on financial firms' lines of business. Currently, we have separate regulators for securities, futures, banks, and insurance. That antediluvian division of labor needs to be scrapped. Under a Twin Peaks structure, one agency would focus on the safety and soundness of financial institutions: the strength of their balance sheets, whom they trade with, and how strong their risk controls are. An agency with this structure would remedy one of the glaring limitations of the SEC—that it has too many lawyers and too few market experts.

The second peak will be more familiar. It would focus on business conduct and investor protection, otherwise known as lying, cheating, inadequate disclosure, and manipulation. This would encompass much of what the SEC is currently supposed to be doing. It would go after big targets and not monkey around with dinky companies and small-time insider-trading issues.

The Twin Peaks model has good-cop, bad-cop appeal. The safety-and-soundness regulator can work with firms to make sure they are solid or else the enforcer will come in. And we should consider a third peak as well: one with responsibility for surveying systemic risk. It would monitor the safety and soundness of the entire financial system, rather than assess it on a company-by-company basis.

One debate—sometimes drawn as a Europe-vs.-U.S. argument—is about whether we should reorder regulation based on broad "principles" rather than strict "rules." This is a red herring, despite the energy expended on it. Rules come from principles, after all. Whatever we have, it needs to be enforced.

Across-the-Board Regulation

In remaking the regulatory architecture, we will need to update the regulatory mandate to deal with 21st-century financial products. Accounting rules should be tightened to prevent anything from being moved off the balance sheet unless there is a true sale of the assets. No entity or instrument should be untouched by some form of regulation.

Regulators need to monitor positions taken by banks, other financial institutions, and major investors, including hedge funds. To its credit, the SEC did attempt in recent years a modest hedge fund registration requirement. The courts struck it down. Congress will have to expand the regulatory mandate to include private investment partnerships, or at least those of a certain size.

Clearly, the regulators will need new powers. We must install higher capital requirements for all financial institutions. Given the disastrous incompetence of the rating agencies, Congress will have to undertake the enormous task of decoupling our regulatory framework from its dependence on ratings. Right now, ratings are written into the fabric of thousands of laws and regulations. Instead, market prices should be used.

There is wide consensus, as there should be, that derivatives [contracts that set prices on assets or futures trading] will be brought under the umbrella. In the 1990s, the definitive fight was over the regulation of derivatives. Brooksley Born, then the head of the CFTC, pushed to regulate them. [Former Federal Reserve chairman] Alan Greenspan, [former U.S. secretary of the Treasury] Robert Rubin, and [director of the White House's National Economic Council] Lawrence Summers fought her. She was right. It's encouraging that people like former SEC commissioner [Arthur] Levitt, who sided with the crowd that argued that regulation would plunge the market into legal chaos, are now having second thoughts. Let's hope the same is true for Summers, who is now in Obama's inner circle, "I have regrets that I didn't use that as an opportunity to say, 'Wait a second, maybe it will create uncertainty, but what about going forward? And what about mandating a clearinghouse?'" Levitt says. "I could have and should have, and I regret not doing it."

Keeping Boardrooms Scared

Other problems are thornier. Can we do something about outrageous compensation for executives and Wall Street? Can we prevent institutions from becoming too big to fail or, worse, too interconnected to fail? Right now, unfortunately, regulators are encouraging mergers, giving us a land of one-eyed institutions buying blind ones. They have to be followed by a complete rethinking of our capital requirements. Stronger capital requirements might help with excessive bonuses too. They will make financial firms more stable, less profitable, and therefore more parsimonious with their own employees in order to leave more for shareholders.

Too Many Regulators, Not Enough Coordination

Largely incompatible with [evolving] market developments is the current system of functional regulation, which maintains separate regulatory agencies across segregated functional lines of financial services, such as banking, insurance, securities, and futures. A functional approach to regulation exhibits several inadequacies, the most significant being the fact that no single regulator possesses all of the information and authority necessary to monitor systemic risk, or the potential that events associated with financial institutions may trigger broad dislocation or a series of defaults that affect the financial system so significantly that the real economy is adversely affected. In addition, the inability of any regulator to take coordinated action throughout the financial system makes it more difficult to address problems related to financial market stability.

US Department of the Treasury,
The Department of the Treasury Blueprint
for a Modernized Financial Regulatory Structure.
Washington, DC: Department of the Treasury,
March 2008.

But a revitalized regulatory sector won't be enough. We need more dissidents. We need to make the world a safer place for short sellers to criticize companies. Regulators should publicly praise short sellers, rather than periodically ban their activities. Critics and whistleblowers, no matter how self-motivated, should be regularly consulted about suspicious companies, not dismissed as cranks once they expose wrongdoing.

And then we need to bring back plaintiffs' lawyers. In the past decade and a half, Republicans not only weakened regulation but also led an attack on these lawyers. Corporate America hated them—and why not? They seem like parasites, ready to pounce on every corporate mistake. But they are vital to keeping capital markets functioning because they keep boardrooms scared. Frank Partnoy, a University of San Diego law professor and prescient critic of the fragile financial markets, says that "it's crucial that standards not stand alone and they be enforced with real teeth. We need public enforcement and private litigation."

The current catastrophe presents us with an opportunity. But the Obama administration and a [chairman of the House Financial Services Committee] Barney Frank-led congressional effort have to be aggressive and ambitious. Reforms can always be scaled back if they overshoot the mark. But the reform-minded cannot enter the debate in a defensive crouch. As new chief of staff Rahm Emanuel says, Don't let a crisis go to waste.

> "We need an FDIC-style resolution authority that can do for the shadow banking system what the FDIC [Federal Deposit Insurance Corporation] does for banks."

Government Should Oversee the Shadow Banking System

Stephen Spruiell and Kevin Williamson

In the following viewpoint, Stephen Spruiell and Kevin Williamson argue that the government must oversee the shadow banking system that deals in risky investments outside mainstream banks. According to the authors, these nontraditional institutions should be subject to regulations imposed by a government entity similar to the Federal Deposit Insurance Corporation. This new overseer should ensure that the shadow banks possess enough capital to back volatile trades and have a predetermined plan for bank failure that would inform traders of the risks and absolve taxpayers of the responsibility of bailing out these banks if they do fail. While Spruiell and Williamson attest that these measures are needed to avoid another catastrophic financial crisis, they also insist that the government-supported mortgage enterprises known as Freddie Mac and Fannie Mae be held to similar con-

Stephen Spruiell and Kevin Williamson, "Resolve to Reform," *National Review*, April 5, 2010. Reprinted with permission.

straints so that taxpayers will never again be forced to prop up these organizations in case of future financial failure. Stephen Spruiell is a staff reporter for National Review Online; *Kevin Williamson is the managing editor of* National Review.

As you read, consider the following questions:

1. Under what agency's jurisdiction should the new shadow banking regulatory institution fall, according to Spruiell and Williamson?

2. What are counter-cyclical capital requirements, as the authors explain?

3. What is the purpose of the "automatic trigger" proposal of Spruiell and Williamson's plan?

What was so bad about the bailouts [to failing banks and car companies in 2008 and 2009]? Everything, except that they sort of worked, at least as a short-term patch-up and a bid for time. But that time is running out, and we should now start thinking about the next crisis, and the next—and how to mitigate what cannot be avoided in the post-TARP [Troubled Asset Relief Program] era.

The really offensive thing about the bailouts was the prevailing sense of adhocracy—that Congress and the White House and the Treasury and the Fed [Federal Reserve] were more or less making things up as they went along. This bank got rescued, that one didn't. This firm got a bailout on generous terms, that one got the pillory. [CEO of Lehman Brothers] Dick Fuld got vilified, [former president of the Federal Reserve Bank of New York] Tim Geithner got made Treasury secretary.

It didn't have to be that way: We have a pretty good system for regulating traditional banks and, when necessary, for taking over failed banks and "resolving" them—taking care of depositors and sorting out losses among creditors and shareholders. The Federal Deposit Insurance Corporation [FDIC] is one of the few players in the recent crisis that have acquitted themselves reasonably well. No American depositor lost a dime from his savings account, checks cleared, and everyone's ATM card kept working. The FDIC works as well as it does because there is not much adhocracy in its approach—terms and practices are defined in advance, and its operations are pre-funded through insurance premiums charged to the banks whose deposits it insures.

Policing the Shadow Banking Industry

But we also have a shadow banking system: a menagerie of hedge funds, structured-investment vehicles, non-depository investment banks, and other intermediaries that shuffle money between borrowers, lenders, and investors outside of traditional banks. Before we can get our economy fully un-TARPed, un-Fannied [referring to Fannie Mae, the Federal National Mortgage Association], and un-Freddied [referring to Freddie Mac, the Federal Home Loan Mortgage Corporation], we need an FDIC-style resolution authority that can do for the shadow banking system what the FDIC does for banks: police safety and soundness and, when necessary, take troubled institutions into custody and disassemble them in an orderly manner.

Some free-marketers will protest that such a resolution authority promises to be just another failed federal regulator, that we should "let markets work." But the bailouts have proved beyond any doubt that "too big to fail" is a durable feature of Washington's thinking about finance—the reality is that an immaculate free-market solution is not in the works. It's rather a question of what sort of regulation we are going to have and who is going to be doing it. We don't expect the new resolution authority to be perfect, but if its powers are well defined and reasonably insulated from electoral politics, it could prove as useful as the FDIC at stemming panic and containing spillovers into the real economy.

The new authority probably should be under the jurisdiction of the Federal Reserve [the Fed], though its activities and the Fed's traditional monetary-policy functions should be walled off from each other. Why the Fed? It has a great deal of financial expertise and knowledge at its disposal, and it is not headed by a cabinet secretary with an eye on the next election. The Fed's haughty independence, for many a source of irritation and suspicion, is in fact its great virtue. It has made its mistakes—keeping interest rates too low for too long, and thereby helping to inflate the housing bubble—but an obsession with short-term politics is not one of them. The FDIC has enough to do, and neither Treasury nor Commerce nor any other cabinet agency should be trusted with the broad powers that any effective resolution authority would have to command.

Drafting Plans for Bank Failure

The institutions that make up the shadow banking system are a diverse and complicated lot: If traditional banking is a game of checkers, this is 3-D chess on dozens of boards at the same time. It is therefore likely that the regulators will lack the expertise to establish appropriate, timely resolution programs for the complex institutions they are expected to govern. The solution to that problem is found in Columbia finance professor Charles Calomiris's proposal that every TBTFI—Too Big to Fail Institution—coming under the new agency's jurisdiction be required to establish and maintain, in advance, its own resolution plan, which would be subject to regulatory approval.

Such a plan—basically, a pre-packaged bankruptcy—would make public detailed information about the distribution of losses in the event of an institutional failure—in other words, who would take how much of a haircut if the bank or fund were to find itself in dire straits. This would be a substantial improvement on the political favor-jockeying that marked the government's intervention in General Motors, for instance, or the political limbo that saw Lehman doing nothing to save itself while waiting to be rescued by a Washington bailout that never came. The authority's main job would be to keep up with the resolution plans and, when necessary, to execute them.

Like the FDIC, the new resolution authority should be pre-funded, its day-to-day operations and its trust fund underwritten by insurance premiums charged to the institutions it oversees. This in itself might have a useful dampening effect: Institutions not wishing to fall under the resolution authority's jurisdiction, thereby becoming subject to the expenses and inconvenience associated with it, would have an incentive to moderate the size and complexity of their operations, which would be a good thing in many cases. Unlike TARP, the authority's trust fund should be treated as what it is—capital backing an insurance program—and restricted by statute from being used as a political slush fund. Being funded by the financial institutions themselves, it would not be subject to the whims of congressional appropriators.

Adjusting Capital Reserves and Setting Triggers

Taking a fresh regulatory approach would give us the opportunity to enact some useful reforms at the same time. At present, capital requirements—the amount of equity and other assets financial firms are required to hold in proportion to their lending—are static: X cents in capital for every $1 in, for example, regular mortgage loans. This makes them "procyclical," meaning that, during booms, banks suddenly find themselves awash in capital as their share prices and the value of their assets climb, with the effect that they can secure a lot more loans with the assets they already have on the books. But the requirements are pro-cyclical on the downside, too: During recessions, declining share and asset prices erode

A Former Securities and Exchange Commission Chairman Argues for Regulation

Products and practices that develop outside the traditional regulatory structure are not inherently harmful, but they do present the potential for very significant risks to develop as they grow outside of regulators' field of vision and authority to act. Federal regulators naturally cannot be expected to oversee effectively those sectors of the financial system that are not fully visible to them. Moreover, "shadow banking" activities heighten the risk that regulators will be put in the position of reacting to market problems, rather than anticipating them. The principal strategy for regulators to combat this possibility is to identify and prioritize risks before they become extreme or systemically troubling.

William H. Donaldson,
Testimony Before the Financial Crisis Inquiry Commission,
May 5, 2010. www.fcic.gov.

banks' capital base, hamstringing their operations and making financial contractions even worse. Instead, we should use counter-cyclical capital requirements: During booms, the amount of capital required to back each dollar in lending should increase on a pre-defined schedule, helping to put the brakes on financial bubbles and to tamp down irrational exuberance. During downturns, capital requirements should be loosened on a pre-defined schedule, to facilitate lending and to keep banks from going into capital crises for mere accounting reasons. But these counter-cyclical capital requirements should begin from a higher baseline: The shadow banking system exists, in no small part, to skirt traditional capital requirements, and its scanty capital cushions helped make the recent crisis much worse than it had to be.

One other aspect of the FDIC that should be incorporated into the new resolution authority: automatic triggers. The FDIC Improvement Act ensures that the agency has relatively little regulatory discretion: If a bank fails to satisfy certain standards, the FDIC is not only empowered to move in and resolve it, but required to do so. Likewise, the resolution authority should have relatively little leeway in its operations. More than the FDIC, perhaps, due to the variety and complexity of the institutions it will be expected to oversee—but not much more. What is most important is that its rules, processes, and standards be well defined in advance—before the next crisis, and the next opportunity for the ad hoc [impromptu] shenanigans that made TARP the hate totem it is.

Only after the new resolution authority is set up can we really untangle ourselves from TARP and the rest of the bailout regime. That is because many of the institutions still being propped up under bailout protocols are weak, and some of them probably are going to fail. Nobody knows which ones, though the amalgamation of corporate blight that is [financial services company] GMAC is an excellent candidate for extinction.

Addressing Government Failures

A special situation, one that probably would exceed the new authority's resources, is the sorry case of Fannie Mae and Freddie Mac. The government-sponsored (now government-owned) enterprises [GSEs] present a real obstacle to returning to a more normal economy. But the first step is relatively straightforward: The government should start by admitting that it is on the hook for all of Fannie and Freddie's losses, not just the $100 billion it has already loaned the companies. The White House still is not accounting for Fannie and Freddie the way it accounts for other federal entities. According to one estimate, Fannie and Freddie's liabilities total $6.3 trillion, every dollar of which is now the taxpayers' potential problem.

Policy makers are understandably reluctant to add such an enormous sum to the national balance sheet, but they could start by accounting for the $300 billion the Congressional Budget Office says it costs to insure the agencies' liabilities against the possibility of default over the next ten years. Adding Fannie and Freddie to budget calculations would, we hope, pressure policy makers to reduce taxpayer exposure to the GSEs by winding down their large portfolios and breaking them up—instead of doing what they are currently doing, which is close to the opposite of that.

Of course, these are our ideal reforms, and they bear only a coincidental resemblance to those that [US senator] Chris Dodd and other congressional panjandrums are bandying about. Dodd's resolution authority would leave too much discretion to politicians to offer insolvent firms permanent life support, Fannie- and Freddie-style, rather than force them into orderly liquidation.

Other proposals we've seen emerge from Congress look more like reorganization than reform, reminding us of the man who wrote, "We tend as a nation to meet any new situation by reorganizing; and a wonderful method it can be for creating the illusion of progress while producing confusion, inefficiency, and demoralization." It is one thing when this reorganizing involves the renaming of some unimportant bureaucracy, but when it comes to financial reform, the illusion of progress is dangerous. Already it can be argued that investors' appetite for risk has returned to pre-crisis levels as government support of the banking system has bolstered the impression that there is no such thing as a bad credit risk on Wall Street. A resolution authority, properly structured, could mitigate this moral hazard by reacquainting the bankers with the prospect of failure and their creditors with the prospect of losses. Whether we will get one is another question entirely.

> *"To avoid further systemic and irreparable meltdowns, legislation must be enacted that requires all standardized derivatives to be guaranteed by well-capitalized clearing facilities and traded on fully transparent and well-regulated exchanges."*

The Government Should Regulate Derivatives Trading

Michael Greenberger

Michael Greenberger is a professor at the University of Maryland School of Law and a former division director at the US Commodity Futures Trading Commission. In the following viewpoint, Michael Greenberger claims that the same financial institutions at the heart of the recent market collapse were heavy traders in derivatives—financial agreements that place values on assets, commodities, or any other tradable item based on expected future prices, interest rates, or debt default. Greenberger maintains that the trading in derivatives has gone unregulated, leading to wild speculation and poor explanation of the risks involved to stockholders in the trading firms. He insists that to avoid another

Michael Greenberger, "Out of the Black Hole: Reining in the Reckless Market in Over-the-Counter Derivatives. (FINANCIAL REFORM)," *The American Prospect*, 21.5, June 2010, pp. A8–A1. Reproduced by permission.

disaster, derivatives trading should be routed through clearing-houses or exchanges where capital can be stored to hedge against contract failures. Greenberger calls on the government to enact such reforms.

As you read, consider the following questions:

1. What does Greenberger insist was the cause of the recent financial crisis?

2. What is another term Greenberger uses for over-the-counter (OTC) derivatives?

3. How does Greenberger suggest avoiding future financial meltdowns?

In September 2008, the United States faced what President Barack Obama called the "most profound economic emergency since the Great Depression." A mortgage crisis begat a credit crisis, shaking the entire financial system and sending the U.S. economy into what has been called the Great Recession.

OTC Derivatives

This crisis was caused in large part by the opaque and un-regulated over-the-counter (OTC) derivatives, or "swaps," market, which was then estimated to have a value of almost $600 trillion, or 10 times the world's gross domestic product. Approximately one-tenth of the unregulated OTC market was made up of the now-infamous credit-default swaps, a product that Wall Street sold to "insure" subprime mortgage investments but which lacked regulation and, therefore, the capital required to support these "guarantees." When subprime investments failed, the "insurance" payments were triggered. Only the multitrillion-dollar U.S. taxpayer interventions to save Wall Street prevented a worldwide depression.

This crisis was the direct result of the deliberate disman-tling of regulatory safeguards. After the collapse of the equity markets and then the banking system between 1929 and 1933, the [Franklin D.] Roosevelt administration drove the passage of the Securities Acts of 1933 and 1934 to regulate securities, and the Commodity Exchange Act of 1936 to regulate futures transactions. These landmark legislative efforts established eight classic regulatory norms to prevent systemic financial collapse in financial markets, including transparency of prices, record-keeping, capital adequacy, full disclosure, anti-fraud and anti-manipulation prohibitions, regulation of intermediaries, private enforcement through litigation, and the federally supervised self-regulation of financial exchanges.

These eight guidelines still govern ordinary stock markets today, and it is noteworthy that malpractices in conventional securities played no role in the 2008 systemic worldwide collapse. These norms had governed the futures markets until 1993 when Wall Street insisted that OTC derivatives be exempt from those traditional regulations. In that year, an accommodating Commodity Futures Trading Commission (CFTC) created an exemption for a limited class of OTC derivatives from classic market regulation.

However, Wall Street almost immediately became dissatisfied with the constraints of the 1993 exemption. Wall Street wanted to sell a far broader range of profitable swaps that could not meet the 1993 restrictions. By 1998, the market grew to over $80 trillion, with swaps dealers conducting most of that business in complete disregard of controlling law.

As a result, in May 1998, the CFTC, under the leadership of then-Chair Brooksley Born, issued a "concept release" inviting public comment on how this multitrillion-dollar unsupervised and opaque market should be regulated. The release was premised on several systemically destabilizing events that had been caused by unregulated OTC swaps.

At the behest of Wall Street, a Republican-controlled Congress passed legislation enjoining Born from this work and then, on the recommendation of the senior [President Bill]

Clinton economic team including among others then-Secretary of the Treasury Larry Summers and Fed [Federal Reserve] Chair Alan Greenspan, rushed through a 262-page rider to an 11,000-page omnibus appropriations bill on Dec. 15, 2000—the last day of a lame-duck session. The rider, the Commodity Futures Modernization Act (CFMA), removed what was by then the $94 trillion OTC-derivative market from all federal regulation.

In one fell swoop, the OTC market was exempt from the traditional market regulatory controls, including capital-adequacy requirements; reporting and disclosure; regulation of intermediaries; supervised self-regulation; and bars on fraud and manipulation. Overnight, the entire OTC market was legitimized as a private market, wholly opaque to financial regulators and market observers.

The Role of OTC Derivatives in the Recent Economic Meltdown

To understand the central role played by OTC derivatives in the recent meltdown, a review of subprime securitization is necessary. In brief, the securitization of subprime mortgage loans evolved to include simple mortgage-backed securities within highly complex collateralized-debt obligations [CDOs]. CDOs packaged huge numbers of mortgage-backed securities, then sliced up those instruments sorted by supposed degree of risk for sale to investors, the so-called tranches. This process, in theory, would offer diversified and graduated risk options to subprime mortgage investors.

However, investors became unmoored from the essential risk underlying loans to non-creditworthy individuals by the continuous reframing of the form of risk (from subprime mortgages to mortgage-backed securities to CDOs); the misleading assurances given by credit-rating agencies; and, most

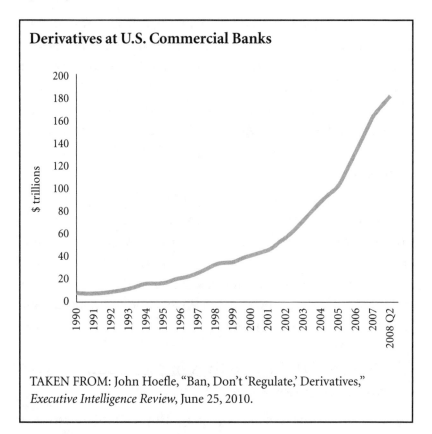

Derivatives at U.S. Commercial Banks

TAKEN FROM: John Hoefle, "Ban, Don't 'Regulate,' Derivatives,"
Executive Intelligence Review, June 25, 2010.

important, the undercapitalized "insurance" offered on CDOs
in the form of credit-default swaps—the poster child for unregulated OTC derivatives.

That "swap" was the exchange by one counter party of a
"premium" for the other counter party's "guarantee" of the financial viability of a CDO. While credit-default swaps have all
the hallmarks of insurance, issuers of these swaps in the insurance industry were urged not to call it "insurance," because
the transactions would be subject to state insurance law, which
would have required, among other protections, adequate capital underpinning the guarantees. Swaps fell into the regulatory
black hole created by the CFMA. Federal regulators had no
knowledge of, or control over, the multitrillion-dollar world of
swaps.

Because a credit-default swap was deemed neither insurance nor a transaction otherwise regulated by the federal government, issuers were not required to set aside adequate capital reserves to stand behind the guarantee of CDOs. The issuers of the swaps were beguiled by the utopian view (supported by ill-considered mathematical algorithms) that housing prices would always go up. They believed that even a borrower who could not afford a mortgage at initial closing would soon be able to extract the appreciating value in the residence to refinance and pay mortgage obligations. Under this utopian view, the writing of a credit-default swap was deemed to be risk-free. The issuers had as their goal the writing of as many swaps as possible to develop the huge cash flow from the "premiums."

To make matters worse, the swaps were deemed to be so free of risk (and so much in demand) that financial institutions began to write "naked" credit-default swaps, offering the guarantee to investors who had no risk in any underlying mortgage-backed instruments. (Under state insurance law, if this had been deemed insurance, rather than a swap, it would be considered insuring someone else's risk, which is flatly banned.) Naked credit-default swaps provided a method to "short" the mortgage-lending market, allowing speculators to place low-cost bets that those who could not afford mortgages would default.

"Synthetic" CDOs

The problem was further aggravated by the development of "synthetic" CDOs. Again, these synthetics were mirror images of "real" obligations, thereby allowing an investor to play "fantasy" securitization: The purchaser of a synthetic CDO did not "own" any of the underlying mortgages or securitized instruments but was simply placing a "bet" on the financial value of a real CDO being mimicked. Synthetic CDOs are also

OTC derivatives and therefore not subject to federal regulation. Synthetic CDOs were also "insured" by unregulated swaps.

Because both naked swaps and synthetic CDOs were nothing more than bets on the viability of the subprime market, at Wall Street's behest, the CFMA banned application of state gambling laws to these transactions.

It is now well established that:

- Issuers of credit-default swaps did not have adequate capital to pay off guarantees as housing prices plummeted, thereby defying the supposedly "risk free" nature of issuing huge guarantees for relatively small premiums.

- Because credit-default swaps are private and bilateral arrangements unknown to federal regulators or market observers, the triggering of such swaps often came as a surprise to both the financial community and regulators.

- As the housing market worsened, new swap obligations were unexpectedly triggered, creating heightened uncertainty about the viability of financial institutions that had, or may have, issued these instruments, thereby leading to the tightening of credit generally.

- The issuance of "naked" credit-default swaps increased exponentially the obligations of swap underwriters, since every time a subprime mortgage defaults there is both the real financial loss and the additional loss derived from failed bets.

- This securitization structure is present not only in the subprime mortgage market but in the prime mortgage market, as well as in commercial real estate, credit-card debt, and automobile and student loans. As of this writing, the financial media is filled with concerns that forfeitures in many of these markets will worsen substantially, thereby triggering many more swaps for which there will almost certainly be insufficient capital to pay the guarantees, thereby restarting the downward cycle that drove the country into recession.

Governmental Regulation

In June 2009, in response to the catastrophic systemic failure caused by unregulated derivatives, the Obama administration issued a white paper proposing that all standardized OTC derivatives be subject to clearing and exchange trading. It proposed that they be overseen in accordance with the traditional dictates of market regulation that had been in place since the New Deal but were abandoned under the CFMA.

The administration also recommended that "all OTC derivatives dealers and all other firms who create large exposures to counter parties should be subject to a robust regime of prudential supervision and regulation," including the imposition of increased capital requirements, business conduct standards, and auditing requirements.

However, on Aug. 11, 2009, the Treasury Department submitted to Congress a specific legislative proposal that substantially undermined the Obama administration's June 2009 stated goal of "bring[ing] the markets for all OTC derivatives . . . into a coherent and coordinated regulatory framework that requires transparency and improves market discipline." On Aug. 17, 2009, CFTC Chair Gary Gensler, in a letter to Congress, critiqued the Treasury's proposed loopholes as being so broad that they could "swallow up the regulation."

While key legislative supporters of the Treasury proposal maintain that its loopholes only exempt 20 percent to 30 percent of the $600 trillion market, respected experts both within and outside of the Obama administration have estimated that almost 60 percent of that market will be unregulated by virtue of only one of the two major loopholes supported by Treasury with state gaming laws unable to stifle any of the rampant "betting" permitted within the unregulated part of the OTC market.

On Dec. 11, 2009, the House passed HR 4173, which contains derivatives language that generally follows the August 2009 Treasury proposal. As of this writing, Sen. Blanche Lincoln has, to the surprise of many observers, just circulated a bill that either eliminates or substantially limits the Treasury loopholes. The Democratic Senate majority now appears to support her effort, and President Obama has just warned wary Republicans that any financial-reform bill that does not strictly regulate the OTC market will be vetoed.

Wall Street Must Be Regulated

Unregulated OTC derivatives have been at the heart of systemic or near systemic collapses—from the 1994 bankruptcy of Orange County, California; to the collapse of Long Term Capital Management in 1998; to the bankruptcy of Enron in 2001–2002; to the 2008 subprime meltdown; and now to an emerging European sovereign-debt crisis in which derivatives were used to disguise the extent of debts taken by nations such as Greece. After each crisis, governments worldwide proclaim that the OTC market must be regulated in the same manner as equity markets, which are dwarfed in value by OTC derivatives. However, Wall Street always deflates those aspirations with aggressive lobbying and campaign contributions. The present financial-reform regulatory effort may be the last chance to prevent the kind of crisis that was dodged in 2008—a worldwide depression. Wall Street and its allies must be stopped now.

To avoid further systemic and irreparable meltdowns, legislation must be enacted that requires all standardized derivatives to be guaranteed by well-capitalized clearing facilities and traded on fully transparent and well-regulated exchanges. This is what the Obama administration's June 2009 white paper promised. The president and Congress should be made to stick to that promise, or the world economy will devolve into a black hole with far greater pull than the regulatory black hole that exists for swaps.

"Because properly used derivatives reduce rather than increase financial
risks, bad regulation will increase
rather than reduce overall risk in the
economy."

Government Should Not Overregulate Derivatives Trading

David M. Mason

*Some observers have blamed the trading of derivatives—finan-
cial contracts concerning future prices or other expected market
outcomes—for the economic collapse that hit the United States
in 2008. Though intended to spread risk, many critics argue that
derivatives spread disaster when losses sink buyers and sellers
equally. In the wake of the crisis, politicians have called for reform of the derivatives market. In the following viewpoint, David
M. Mason cautions against imposing blanket reform. In his
opinion, derivatives are useful ways for companies to spread risk,
and Mason argues that by imposing new regulation on such
trades, banking institutions will be less likely to deal in derivatives. As a result, failures in specific commodities or futures will
compound damage to these financial powerhouses and likely*

David M. Mason, "The 'Comprehensive' Problem with Derivatives Regulation," Heritage
Foundation 2862, April 15, 2010. Reprinted with permission.

cripple the economy. Mason suggests that lawmakers carefully consider what problems with derivatives might have abetted the financial crisis and draft targeted legislation instead of enacting comprehensive mandates. David M. Mason is a visiting fellow at the Thomas A. Roe Institute for Economic Policy Studies at the Heritage Foundation, a public policy think tank.

As you read, consider the following questions:

1. Why does Mason believe that derivatives trading had little impact on the fall of Lehman Brothers in 2008?

2. What government agencies already regulate derivatives trading, as Mason reports?

3. Why do some derivatives—such as interest rate swaps— pose no systemic risk, according to the author?

Persuaded that lax regulation of financial derivatives [financial agreements based on expected future assets] contributed to the 2008 financial crisis, policy makers in Congress and the [Barack] Obama administration have adopted a knee-jerk solution: regulate everything.

The Obama administration has proposed and the House Financial Services [Committee] and Senate Committee [on Banking, Housing and Urban Affairs] have each approved schemes for regulating derivatives that differ in many details. But the proposals agree on the most significant point: that derivatives regulation must be "comprehensive." By "comprehensive," regulators mean that every financial product, every buyer, every seller, every intermediary, and every transaction must be regulated unless expressly exempted by statute or decree.

The premise supporting the blanket regulatory diktat— that every derivative contract poses systemic risk to the financial system—is unproven, the application overly broad, and the resulting bureaucratic burden excessively heavy. Congress should:

- Resist simplistic calls for "more regulation" until proponents demonstrate that particular types of derivatives caused or intensified the financial crisis;

- Apply any new regulation to the derivative products, institutions, or market mechanisms that caused economic harm; and

- Tailor regulation to address specific problems or harms identified.

Did Derivatives Cause the Financial Crisis?

The differing financial reform proposals passed by the House and awaiting consideration in the Senate would impose comprehensive derivatives regulation by subjecting derivatives now traded over-the-counter (OTC) by banks and other financial institutions to regulation by the Commodity Futures Trading Commission (CFTC) and/or the Securities and Exchange Commission (SEC).

Proponents of additional derivatives regulation apparently view the need for more regulation as self-evident. CFTC Chairman Gary Gensler analogizes derivatives regulation to building codes to prevent fire—without, however, explaining what role derivatives played in the financial conflagration.

In the wake of the 1987 stock market crash, then New York Stock Exchange [NYSE] Chairman Richard Phelan blamed a new and fast-growing derivative—S&P 500 Index futures—traded on the Chicago Mercantile Exchange. Phelan's charge sparked an outcry for more regulation. But after the crisis subsided, careful studies concluded that the 1987 crash was caused not by derivatives but by macroeconomic factors and government policy mistakes such as anti-takeover legislation. To the extent that flaws in markets intensified the crash, the problems were in the NYSE's own antiquated order fulfillment system.

In the wake of [investment banking firm] Lehman Brothers' 2008 bankruptcy, former Lehman CEO Dick Fuld blamed a new and fast-growing derivative—credit default swaps (CDS)—for his firm's failure, fueling calls to regulate CDS. But after a year's review, Lehman's bankruptcy examiner found that Lehman failed due to its own poor business decisions. There was also evidence that Fuld himself approved misleading financial statements. Lehman's derivatives positions represented only about 3.3 percent of its net assets, and the examiner found its derivatives trades were reasonable and more carefully monitored than other asset classes.

There is legitimate debate about the role that credit default swaps (CDS) and other derivatives played in the 2008 financial crisis. But as Phelan and Fuld's inaccurate accusations show, initial claims can be misleading. Awaiting the conclusions of the Financial Crisis Inquiry Commission and other careful studies would empower Congress to make informed decisions rather than simply throwing a regulatory blanket over anything called a derivative. Congress and the CFTC cannot design a useful "building code" until they understand the role, if any, that derivatives played in the crisis.

All Derivatives Are Not the Same

Derivatives are financial instruments used to transfer risk from a party seeking to "hedge" (limit) risk to a party willing—for a fee—to assume the risk. Risks transferred may be related to prices (whether they rise, fall, or fluctuate), interest rates, exchange rates, or they may be related to whether a third party will pay its debts.

Derivatives play a productive economic role by allowing firms to plan based on stable economic factors while transferring the risk (including the potential reward) of economic disruptions to others who are willing and able to assume it. The term *derivative* applies to this diverse set of products because their value is determined by reference to another underlying product or transaction.

Some derivatives, such as commodity or stock futures, are regulated by the CFTC or SEC. Other derivatives related to interest rates, foreign exchange, and debt (called "financial derivatives") are traded largely OTC among banks, whose operations are regulated by the Federal Reserve and other banking agencies.

Financial derivatives differ significantly from commodity derivatives in their characteristics, uses, and markets. For instance, most nonfinancial derivatives involve a single payment followed by settlement at the end of the contract term, such as a commodity future that sets in advance the price to be paid when products are delivered months later. In contrast, many financial derivatives involve long-term streams of payments between parties, which is more akin to a typical lending relationship.

There is no suggestion that interest rate swaps (the largest category of OTC financial derivatives) or foreign exchange swaps played any role in the financial disruptions of 2008. Yet the House and Senate proposals extend regulatory rules for physical commodities and stocks to these bank-based products. Wantonly extending commodity-focused regulation to financial derivatives applies the wrong tool in the wrong application. The result would be ineffective regulation damaging everything involved. For instance, commodity and stock futures are normally settled by physical delivery whereas most financial derivatives are settled by cash payments—often over an extended period.

"Comprehensive" Regulation Is Not Appropriate or Necessary

Gensler is anxious to impose a clearing mandate, among other rules, on OTC derivatives. The mandate would require most derivative contracts to be settled through a clearinghouse rather than directly between the parties. The clearinghouse acts as a middleman, receiving and distributing payments after a contract is formed between the original parties. This arrangement arguably reduces the risk that a contract will not be honored.

What percentage of OTC derivatives contracts can be cleared, at what cost, is critical to determining whether a clearing mandate is appropriate. Gensler asserts that 75 percent of OTC derivatives could be centrally cleared. Gensler's source, however, is not an analysis by his agency, a peer-reviewed study, or a market survey. The only evidence Gensler cites is a ballpark estimate by a single executive whom Gensler never names.

An agency head owes Congress and the public more than an uncorroborated opinion from an unnamed source to justify a massive expansion of regulatory authority. Gensler has not bothered to address this question rigorously, but he has made up his mind and is eager to issue orders to the market.

Gensler and other Obama administration officials also insist that exemptions to derivatives rules be very narrow. For instance, the Senate Committee [on Banking, Housing and Urban Affairs] bill requires approval from both the principal regulatory agency and certification by the Financial Stability Oversight Council to exempt any end user, swap dealer, bank, non-bank financial institution, security, or other product from derivatives rules. Imposing a duplicative exemption process guarantees that one-size-fits-all mandates will be imposed with little reason.

Uniformity: At What Cost?

The principal justification for regulating derivatives is that they pose "systemic risks" to the financial system. Yet some derivatives, such as interest rate swaps, pose no systemic risk because their values change slowly and their characteristics are well understood. Other derivative types or user categories are so small as to be insignificant to the overall financial system. Gensler acknowledges, for instance, that corporate end users represent only about 9 percent of derivatives transactions, but he argues against their exemption from collateral requirements for no better reason than to uphold the "regulate everything" principle.

Applying ill-designed blanket regulation will make financial derivatives more costly, more difficult to customize, and consequently less widely used. Because properly used derivatives reduce rather than increase financial risks, bad regulation will increase rather than reduce overall risk in the economy.

A Better Response

The Obama administration and committees in Congress propose to regulate financial derivatives with an antiquated scheme designed for physical commodities. This inflexible and damaging mandate is unjustified. Instead, Congress should:

- Consider carefully any evidence that particular types of derivatives caused or intensified the financial crisis;

- Craft regulations to address specific problems rather than imposing blanket mandates; and

- Create rules that encourage rather than discourage risk-mitigating uses of financial derivatives.

Leading derivatives reform proposals amount to little more than a frenzied insistence to do something, anything, to regulate financial derivatives. Proponents must show why particular derivatives need to be more closely regulated and that the schemes they propose will reduce rather than increase risks in financial markets.

"The American financial sector will be reformed, but it should not be at the expense of our local institutions."

Government Reform Will Hurt Small Lenders

Blaine Luetkemeyer

Missouri Republican Blaine Luetkemeyer is a member of the US House of Representatives. In the following viewpoint, he contends that small, community banks did not cause the current financial crisis. Therefore, he argues that sweeping legislation to reform banking in the United States might unfairly penalize these institutions with burdens that will dry up needed credit and restrict lending. Because big financial organizations were taking unnecessary risks and gambling with investors' money, Luetkemeyer believes Congress should target these conglomerations, using legislation to break them up and reduce their overall risk to the economy. He maintains that community banks— which weathered the financial storm due to above-board conduct—should not suffer for the reckless behavior of the Wall Street banks.

Blaine Luetkemeyer, "Wall Street Reform Hurts Main Street Banks," *Washington Times*, May 25, 2010. www.washingtontimes.com. Reproduced by permission.

As you read, consider the following questions:

1. Instead of adding another "layer of regulation," what does Luetkemeyer insist legislators need to do with existing regulating agencies?

2. What bailout proposal, by House Democrats, does Luetkemeyer claim should be scrapped?

3. According to the author, about how much money did taxpayers pay out to bail out Freddie Mac and Fannie Mae?

For more than 60 years, my late father, Bill, spent every day looking into the faces of family farmers and ranchers hoping to realize their dreams as they walked into his bank in St. Elizabeth, Mo. My father understood the importance of community banking the day he started in 1940, and he passed that understanding to me when I later joined him in the family business. In a town of 300 that lacks both a stoplight and significant financial resources, the community always came first in the role of our small bank.

Now the federal government is redefining the role of a community bank in the name of "Wall Street reform." Few people I talk to at home, Republican or Democrat, would argue there is not a need for financial reform, but to achieve real improvements, we must take the time to differentiate between firms whose actions have national and international implications and real systemic risk, and those that service communities by funding small businesses and lending to local families. The American financial sector will be reformed, but it should not be at the expense of our local institutions.

People on Main Street understand that community banks did not cause the financial crisis and that they already carry daunting regulatory burdens. The regulatory reform legislation proposed by the [Barack Obama] administration will subject all banks, regardless of size, to the potentially overreaching rules of another new government agency, placing new rules that have very little to do with correcting the deficiencies that led to the financial crisis. This new bureaucracy would have sweeping examination and enforcement authorities and the ability to restrict consumer access to credit. Big banks may be able to weather the regulatory storm, but some smaller community banks will be unable to stay afloat. The impact of this ill-conceived and dangerous plan will destroy jobs by making it more expensive and difficult for hardworking Americans to thrive in a modern economy built on access to affordable and available credit. In my view, we do not need another layer of regulation. We need the existing regulators just to do their job, and if they will not, then we need to clean house.

If Congress is going to pass meaningful reform legislation in hopes of preventing another financial meltdown, we need to focus more on what is broken and less on changing what already is working. First and foremost, we have to scrap the idea of more government bailouts and the notion that certain institutions are too big to fail—implying that community banks are too small to save. It's my belief that large, failing firms should be unwound by declaring bankruptcy—just like the rest of us—so we are not forced to rely on regulators and taxpayer-funded bailouts to maintain financial stability.

But Senate Democrats have offered reform that makes more bailouts a permanent part of the regulatory arsenal. House Democrats even want to establish a $150 billion permanent bailout fund. The only purpose of such a fund is to pay off creditors of failed financial institutions, leaving the taxpayers as the financial backstop to failed investments. Instead of forcing creditors to internalize their losses and be held accountable for managing their credit risks, the bailout fund permits these creditors to spread their risk and losses across the entire financial system, infecting small banks and individuals and putting our taxpayer dollars at risk.

Restricting Loans and Credit at Small Banks

With the threat of regulatory scrutiny and monetary penalties over lending decisions, many banks and—in particular—smaller community banks, will think twice before granting new loans.

Additionally, stricter capital requirements and increased scrutiny over credit decisions will drain credit available to borrowers.

McGladrey & Pullen,
"The Impact of the Financial Reform Act on Banks and Other
Financial Institutions," 2010. http://mcgladrey.com.

My experience as a former bank examiner and community bank officer has shown me that managing risk is one of the most important things a bank, particularly a small community bank, can do. That's why it's poor regulatory business to have the same capital requirement for a bank involved in high-risk lending or heavy concentrations of particular loans as for one that's servicing a broad spectrum of small businesses. After more than 30 years as a community banker, I am certain the current approach to banking reform and risk isn't balanced and will give the big banks an economic advantage, which, in the end, will cause credit to be restricted and be more costly to the small business borrowers.

And like the bailouts, any reform must address the real causes of the problem, and that includes the mortgage crisis. The legislation in the Senate, much like the legislation passed by the House in December [2009], does nothing to reform or even regulate Fannie Mae [the Federal National Mortgage Association] or Freddie Mac [the Federal Home Loan Mortgage

Corporation], the government-sponsored enterprises that contributed extensively to the U.S. banking turmoil. Communities across our nation understand that Fannie and Freddie recklessly abused their then implicit government guarantee, and taxpayers have forked out more than $145 billion to bail them out and will continue to put billions more into these failed entities before the losses stop. While Democrats continue to defend their failures, House Republicans have introduced several bills to help protect taxpayers and return Fannie and Freddie to working order and off the government payroll.

Community banks, like the one where I worked, understand that looking a person in the eye, offering a firm handshake and making sure that no additional burdens are placed on our neighbor's dream is the recipe for a growing and prosperous community. Anything less than that constitutes failure, and that's exactly where the Democrats' plan for financial regulatory reform will lead our financial system, including our community banks and our economy as a whole.

> *"Though the financial crisis hurt the megabanks' profits . . . , it did nothing to weaken their political power."*

Big Banks Have Too Much Political Power

Simon Johnson and James Kwak

In the following viewpoint, Simon Johnson and James Kwak argue that huge Wall Street banking institutions have too much political power. In the authors' opinion, years of deregulation have helped large banks grow to the point where they disproportionately influence the economy. Along with this growth persists a belief among policy makers and average citizens that Wall Street gains are a sign of a strong economy. Johnson and Kwak counter that this mantra is simply a means for banks to legitimize their growth and convince lawmakers to refrain from interfering with moneymaking. Fueled by a strong political lobby, big banks now regularly influence politics and protect themselves from proposed regulations, Johnson and Kwak maintain. The authors warn that even in the current crisis, Wall Street banks are finding ways of deflecting blame for wrongdoing and continuing with business as usual. Simon Johnson is a former chief economist at the International Monetary Fund. James Kwak is a

Simon Johnson and James Kwak, "Too Big for Us to Fail," *American Prospect*, April 26, 2010. Reproduced by permission.

law student and cofounder of a software company. Johnson and Kwak are the coauthors of 13 Bankers: The Wall Street Take-over and the Next Financial Meltdown, *a work that investigates the rise of big banks.*

As you read, consider the following questions:

1. What three legislative acts do Johnson and Kwak mention as contributing to the growth of megabanks between 1982 and 2000?

2. According to the authors, who wrote the recent draft legislation aimed at reforming derivatives?

3. Citing Center for Responsive Politics data, how much money do the authors say the finance, insurance, and real estate sector spent on congressional lobbying in 2009?

Financial regulatory reform was on few people's minds when Barack Obama launched his presidential campaign in February 2007. But with the near collapse of the global financial system in 2008, leading to high unemployment and high government deficits for years to come, it became frighteningly obvious that something had to change. However, in one respect—the politics of financial reform—nothing has changed.

The Obama administration has led the push to reform the financial system. We agree with many of its proposals, including a strong Consumer Financial Protection Agency, dedicated oversight of systemic risk, and new requirements to move derivatives onto exchanges and central clearinghouses. At the same time, we do not think the administration has gone far enough to curb the behavior of "too big to fail" institutions and mitigate the risk that they pose to the financial system and the economy. But these reasonable debates over how the regulatory system *should* be overhauled are peripheral to a more fundamental issue: the political power of the financial sector, which determines how the regulatory system *will* be overhauled, if at all.

Lax Regulations Helped Grow Megabanks

The growth of the megabanks, the rapid spread of financial "innovation," the excessive risk taking of the past decade, and the financial crisis were not purely economic phenomena. They had deeply political roots, in the deregulatory philosophy of the [Ronald] Reagan Revolution and the ideology of finance spawned by free market economists. And the big profits on Wall Street were made possible in the halls of power in Washington.

From the Garn-St. Germain [Depository Institutions] Act of 1982 (substantially deregulating savings and loan institutions) to the Gramm-Leach-Bliley Act [the Financial Services Modernization Act] of 1999 (allowing combined commercial and investment banking) and the Commodity Futures Modernization Act of 2000 (permitting largely unrestricted trading in derivatives), Congress relaxed the regulatory constraints that had housebroken the financial industry since the 1930s, while failing to establish effective oversight of custom derivatives. The Federal Reserve spent the 1990s relaxing constraints on commercial banks and the 2000s neglecting to enforce consumer protection laws against predatory mortgage lenders. In 2004, the Securities and Exchange Commission relaxed capital requirements for major investment banks in exchange for the power to oversee them through the Consolidated Supervised Entity Program—a program that failed spectacularly with both Bear Stearns and Lehman Brothers.

Big Banks Gain Big Influence

The core failure of the past 30 years was not that Wall Street financial engineers thought of clever ways to make money; that is absolutely par for the course. The failure was that Wall Street was able to gain sufficient influence in Washington to win favorable policies from Congress, regulators, and both Democratic and Republican administrations. The banks earned their political power the old-fashioned way, through campaign contributions and lobbying expenditures; the financial sector was the primary source of campaign money for the past two decades, and its contributions grew disproportionately rapidly over the period. More important, the popularization and spread of the ideology of finance meant that politicians and government officials increasingly came to *sincerely believe* that what was good for Wall Street was good for America.

The collapse of Lehman Brothers and the near failures of Morgan Stanley and Goldman Sachs—chronicled in detail in Andrew Ross Sorkin's *Too Big to Fail*—should have shaken this belief. The recent report by Anton Valukas, the examiner in the Lehman bankruptcy, revealing a history of (at best) misleading accounting and lax government oversight, should have obliterated its remains. But although Washington is more willing to regulate now than in years past, one thing has emphatically not changed: the power of the banking industry to fight back. All of the techniques honed over the past few decades have been evident in full force over the past year [2010].

One technique is the use of complexity. The modern financial world is complex, and most of the experts work on or for Wall Street. When it comes time to draft new legislation governing highly technical topics such as derivatives, those insiders have a clear advantage over most congressional staffers. In November [2009], [journalist] William Greider described how derivatives dealers wrote the draft legislation reforming regulation of derivatives and funneled it into Congress via conservative Democrats on the House Financial Services Committee. Administration officials such as Gary Gensler, chair of the U.S. Commodity Futures Trading Commission, have fought to close the loopholes in that draft bill, but the Senate bill introduced by Christopher Dodd in March [2010] contains its own new exemptions.

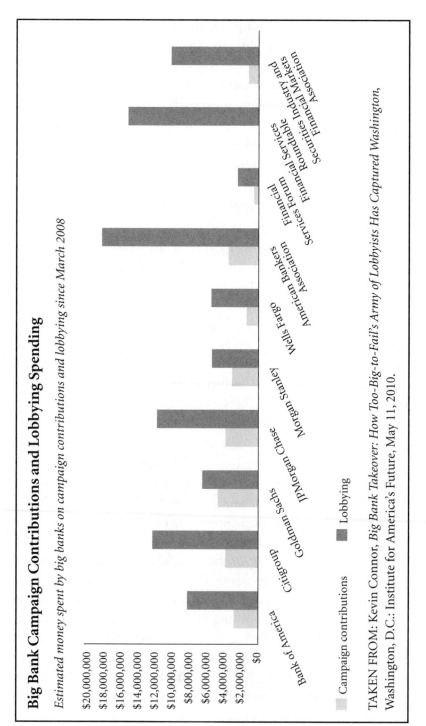

Big Bank Campaign Contributions and Lobbying Spending

Estimated money spent by big banks on campaign contributions and lobbying since March 2008

Campaign contributions ▪ Lobbying

Bank of America
Citigroup
Goldman Sachs
JPMorgan Chase
Morgan Stanley
Wells Fargo
American Bankers Association
Financial Services Forum
Financial Services Roundtable
Securities Industry and Financial Markets Association

$20,000,000
$18,000,000
$16,000,000
$14,000,000
$12,000,000
$10,000,000
$8,000,000
$6,000,000
$4,000,000
$2,000,000
$0

TAKEN FROM: Kevin Connor, *Big Bank Takeover: How Too-Big-to-Fail's Army of Lobbyists Has Captured Washington,* Washington, D.C.: Institute for America's Future, May 11, 2010.

Another technique is to hide behind "ordinary people." During the boom years, one major argument for financial innovation was that it increased homeownership—a tenet subscribed to by both the Bill Clinton and George W. Bush administrations. Early in 2009, the American Bankers Association opposed legislation giving bankruptcy judges the power to modify the terms of mortgages on the grounds that it would "make home loans more expensive and less available for consumers." As the legislative battle heated up in the summer and fall, the financial lobby rolled out "end users" of derivatives—corporations that use options or futures for legitimate hedging of risks—to testify against regulatory reform. The U.S. Chamber of Commerce pitched in with advertisements warning ominously that stronger consumer protection rules would be bad for American business.

The framing of the argument has changed. It is no longer that unrestricted finance will bring benefits to all Americans; it is now that restricting finance will actively cause harm to Americans. In effect, the financial sector is attempting to hold the economy hostage yet again. Handcuff the banks, for example, by making it harder to increase interest rates on credit card customers, and many people will lose access to credit. Or so the threat goes.

The Banking Lobby

Even as the ideology of deregulation has been exposed as a failure, the banks and their political allies are still invoking the bogeyman of big government to fight off financial reform. Political consultant Frank Luntz clearly spelled out the strategy to demonize reform by branding it as more bureaucracy, bailouts, and special interest loopholes. This has created the Orwellian [referring to author George Orwell's idea of government interference in a free society] specter of Republicans introducing special interest loopholes into reform legislation (such as an exemption for automobile dealers from the proposed Consumer Financial Protection Agency, introduced by Rep. John Campbell, a Republican) and then criticizing the same legislation for its loopholes.

Journalists Ryan Grim and Arthur Delaney have documented how Democrats have placed new, relatively conservative members of Congress from Republican-leaning districts on the House Financial Services Committee, because it increases their ability to raise money. Unfortunately, the effect was to create an influential bloc of banking-friendly *Democrats* on the committee, who allied with Republicans on certain issues to weaken financial reform legislation, against the wishes of committee chair Barney Frank.

At the same time, lobbying by the financial sector has reached record levels. According to data collected by the Center for Responsive Politics, the finance, insurance, and real estate sector spent over $463 million on lobbying in 2009, the most ever. (The banking and securities industries were responsible for $144 million of that total, also a record.) Even Citigroup spent over $5 million on lobbying—although the government was its largest shareholder.

In sum, though the financial crisis hurt the megabanks' profits (for a quarter or two, at least), it did nothing to weaken their political power. If anything, increased concentration only increased the stature and influence of the survivors, and the Supreme Court's 2009 decision in *Citizens United*[1] put politicians on notice that corporate influence over politics is likely only to grow.

Real Reform Will Require Grassroots and Government Action

What would it take to curb the political power of the financial sector? Grassroots campaigns, such as the Move Your Money campaign to take money out of large banks, could have a

---

1. *Citizens United v. Federal Election Commission* eliminated campaign spending limits for corporations.

small impact. New laws or constitutional amendments to restrict the role of money in politics would certainly help. Restrictions on compensation, by making banking less lucrative and less alluring, would help reduce the ideological hegemony of Wall Street. Breaking up the megabanks, by increasing competition and increasing the costs of collective action, would help most of all.

Ultimately this will come down to a battle of ideas, one that will take years to win. As long as people think that finance is inherently good and big finance is inherently better, Washington will remain easily swayed by Wall Street. The political power of the banking industry is not simply a product of its deep pockets; imagine, for example, how much harder and more expensive it would be for the tobacco industry to dominate Washington. Tobacco once had far more power than it does today. Its diminished influence shows the influence of citizen and government efforts—a story that should give us hope that finance can also be constrained.

We should not think of finance as the pride and joy of our economy but as something like a regulated utility (an industry on which the economy depends but that should be watched over carefully) and something like big tobacco (an industry that makes toxic products with huge negative externalities). Shifting the conventional wisdom in this direction will be a prerequisite for fundamental reform of both the financial system and the political system in the long term.

Periodical and Internet Sources Bibliography

The following articles have been selected to supplement the diverse views presented in this chapter.

Charles W. Calomiris	"Financial Reforms We Can All Agree On," *Wall Street Journal*, April 23, 2009.
John Cassidy	"The Volcker Rule," *New Yorker*, July 26, 2010.
Hugo Dixon and Richard Beales	"Europeans Favor Regulating 'Shadow Banks,'" *New York Times*, February 23, 2009.
Economist	"The Uneven Contest," January 22, 2009.
William Greider	"Obama's False Financial Reform," *Nation*, June 19, 2009.
Christine Lagarde	"Financial Reform: No Time to Pull Back," *BusinessWeek*, September 24, 2009.
John Maggs	"Do We Have to Kill the Shadow Banking System?" *National Journal*, May 1, 2009.
Sarah Wallace	"The End of Community Banking," *Wall Street Journal*, June 29, 2010.
Mortimer B. Zuckerman	"7 Fixes for a Market Failure," *U.S. News & World Report*, May 9, 2008.

CHAPTER 3

Will Financial Reform Legislation Be Effective?

Chapter Preface

On Thursday July 15, 2010, the Senate passed the Dodd-Frank Wall Street Reform and Consumer Protection Act after a year of lobbying and debate. The document, twenty-three hundred pages in length, was signed into law the following week by President Barack Obama. Advocates claim the bill will place necessary checks on Wall Street speculation. Critics, on the other hand, charge that the Dodd-Frank bill allows government unprecedented oversight of financial markets, and Representative Jeb Hensarling of Texas warns that "massively expanding the size of government's regulatory bureaucracy with new layers, agencies, and required rule makings does not mean that oversight will get any better."

The Dodd-Frank bill establishes a Consumer Financial Protection Bureau with the mission to monitor lending practices and stop predatory mortgages and abuses involving credit card fees. The government also will gain a Financial Stability Oversight Council that supposedly will watch for systemic risks to the economy and have the power to put failing financial firms into liquidation instead of bailing them out with taxpayer dollars. The council will also have the authority to require big financial firms to keep more capital on hand to back risky ventures and restrict leveraging (buying on debt). Critics worry that the council is not made up of new blood but rather "the same folks who were asleep at the wheel in the run-up to the 2008 meltdown," as Andy Kroll writes in the July 15, 2010, issue of *Mother Jones*.

While these levels of oversight have stirred controversy, the heart of the debate over the reform bill pertains to what regulations have been placed on trading and speculation in financial firms. The Volcker Rule, named after former Federal Reserve chairman Paul Volcker, survived the Senate wrangling in a revised state. The original rule restricted banks from trading stocks, bonds, derivatives, or other securities for their own profit (as opposed to trading to increase the profits of their customers); the final version of the rule stipulates that the banks can only trade up to 3 percent of their capital in transactions that do not enrich customers. The trading market for derivatives—financial instruments that derive their value based on a speculative future value—has also changed due to new regulation. In the past, banks traded derivatives over the counter—that is, without government oversight—to millions of customers who shared the risk or profit when these speculations went up or down in value. Banks collected fees on each transaction and so became middlemen between, say, a mortgage lender in the United States and investors in Saudi Arabia, Germany, and Japan. Sometimes the banks never calculated the risks involved in the derivatives, and even more commonly, buyers had no idea what risk they were sharing because various derivatives could be bundled before they were sold. The new legislation forces banks to trade derivatives through clearinghouses that will inform buyers and sellers of the risks and require all parties to put money up front to hedge against potential market failures. Economist Robert Engle told the Big Think website on July 15, 2010, that "the risks that are taken and not really well disclosed are not going to be as easy to take anymore." The law also requires banks that are backed by the Federal Reserve to divorce most of their trading from their banking activities, meaning that banks will need to use ancillary offices to conduct trades and that market failures will not be bailed out with government money.

Debate continues about whether the final reform bill will be effective at preventing another financial meltdown. However, the disputes that took place during the shaping of the bill reveal the controversial nature of each proposed remedy. The following chapter explores these proposals and the arguments for and against including them in reform legislation.

| *"If a crisis like this again happens, financial firms are going to foot the bill."*

The Financial Reform Bill Will Make Big Business More Responsible

Barack Obama

Barack Obama is the forty-fourth president of the United States and a major proponent of financial reform in response to the recent economic crisis. In the following viewpoint, an address made in his home state of Illinois, the president explains why he believes reform measures are needed and what they will entail in the new congressional reform bill. According to Obama, reckless risk taking on the part of large financial institutions made the economy unstable, leading to a crash that could be righted only through an emergency taxpayer-funded bailout. The president maintains that to avoid another bailout, government reform will curb risky trading, provide shareholders and investors with more information and influence over bank activity, and ensure protection for consumers. He expects that such legislation will force big banks to be more fiscally responsible to Americans and the goal of economic growth.

Barack Obama, Remarks by the President on Wall Street Reform in Quincy, Illinois, April 28, 2010. www.whitehouse.gov. Reproduced by permission.

As you read, consider the following questions:

1. According to Obama, businesses can keep on making money fairly as long as they do what?

2. What reasons does Obama give for strengthening consumer protection policies in the proposed Wall Street reforms?

3. What incentives does Obama claim may have enticed bank executives to take "reckless risks" with investors' money?

When I took office [January 20, 2009], we were in the midst of this historic financial crisis brought on by reckless and irresponsible speculation on Wall Street. That in turn had led to a recession that hammered Main Street across America. And you saw lost jobs and lost homes and lost businesses and downscaled dreams.

The first thing we had to do then was mount an aggressive response—to make sure that this terrible recession didn't turn into another Great Depression. And let's face it, that required some tough steps to stabilize the financial sector. And some of those steps weren't popular. I knew they weren't popular. I've got pollsters. They told me, boy, that's really going to be unpopular. But we made those decisions anyway, because the well-being of millions of Americans depended on them. Even if they didn't poll well, they were the right thing to do. It was the only thing we could do to take those steps. . . .

But, keep in mind, I didn't run for president just to get back to where we were when we started. I want us to do better than we were doing. I want folks to have more opportunity. I want people to have more and better jobs. And I want our young people to be getting better educations and more access to college.

It's time to rebuild our economy on a new foundation so that we've got real and sustained growth. It's time to extend opportunity to every corner of Main Street, in every city and every town and every county in America, so that young people don't feel like they've got to move someplace else to make their way. . . .

It's time to create conditions so that Americans who work hard can gain ground again, and they don't have to take out a bunch of credit card debt. They don't have to endanger their long-term financial future. And that's what—that's at the heart of all our efforts. . . .

And, yes, . . . that's why we finally passed health reform in America[1]—reform that will begin to end some of the worst practices in the insurance industry this year [2010]. So this year, they're going to—they will have to stop dropping you when you get sick. This year, children with preexisting conditions, they've got to be able to buy insurance. This year, some of these lifetime limits that mean that you got insurance but you still end up being bankrupt—those practices are going to end. . . .

This isn't some abstraction. Sometimes, the folks who were fighting us, they made it sound as if, oh, he just wants big government, this—no. I just want people to be able to not go bankrupt and lose their house when they get sick. I just want them not to have—see their premiums doubled. I don't want them to be taken advantage of by insurance companies. I want you to get a fair deal and a fair shake. And that's part of my job as president of the United States of America. . . .

Reckless Risk Taking

Now, speaking of—speaking of you getting a fair shake, that's why we need good old commonsense Wall Street reform. And we need it today. We don't need it next year. We don't need to do another study and examine it. We need it now.

1. The Affordable Health Care for America Act was signed into law by President Barack Obama on March 23, 2010.

And in case you're wondering, let me just take a minute to explain why it's important to you. The crisis we went through, it wasn't part of the normal economic cycle. What happened was you had some people—not all people—there's some very decent people here who are in the financial sector—but you had some people on Wall Street who took these unbelievable risks with other people's money.

They made bets. They were making bets on what was going to happen in the housing market, and they would create these derivatives and all these instruments that nobody understood. But it was basically operating like a big casino. And it was producing big profits and big bonuses for them, but it was all built on shaky economics and some of these subprime loans that had been given out. And because we did not have commonsense rules in place, those irresponsible practices came awfully close to bringing down our entire economy and millions of dreams along with it.

We had a system where some on Wall Street could take these risks without fear of failure, because they keep the profits when it was working, and as soon as it went south, they expected you to cover their losses. So it was one of those heads, they [win]—tails, you lose.

So they failed to consider that behind every dollar that they traded, all that leverage they were generating, acting like it was Monopoly money, there were real families out who were trying to finance a home, or pay for their child's college, or open a business, or save for retirement. So what's working fine for them wasn't working for ordinary Americans. And we've learned that clearly. It doesn't work out fine for the country. It's got to change.

Now, what we're doing—I want to be clear, we're not trying to push financial reform because we begrudge success that's fairly earned. I mean, I do think at a certain point you've made enough money. But part of the American way is you can just keep on making it if you're providing a good product or you're providing a good service. We don't want people to stop fulfilling the core responsibilities of the financial system to help grow the economy.

The Financial System Must Help the Economy Expand

I've said this before. I've said this on Wall Street just last week [in April 2010]. I believe in the power of the free market. And I believe in a strong financial system. And when it's working right, financial institutions, they help make possible families buying homes, and businesses growing, and new ideas taking flight. An entrepreneur may have a great idea, but he may need to borrow some money to make it happen. It would be hard for a lot of us to buy a house—our first house, at least, if we weren't able to take out a mortgage.

So there's nothing wrong with a financial system that helps the economy expand. And there are a lot of good people in the financial industry who are doing things the right way. And it's in our interest when those firms are strong and when they're healthy.

But some of these institutions that operated irresponsibly, they're not just threatening themselves—they threaten the whole economy. And they threaten your dreams, your prospects, everything that you worked so hard to build.

So we just want them to operate in a way that's fair and honest and in the open, so that we don't have to go through what we've already gone through. We want to make sure the financial system doesn't just work for Wall Street, but it works for Main Street, too. . . .

Now, let me explain to you what this reform should look like, because one of the things you discover when you get to Washington is what's black is white and what's up is down and sometimes people will—

Audience member: Lie.

I didn't say lie, but—they will tell stories about what's going on. So let me just be very clear in terms of what we're proposing on financial reform. First—and I know this is important to you because it's important to me—we're going to make sure the American taxpayer is never again on the hook when a Wall Street firm fails. Never again. We don't want to see another bailout. That's what this reform does.

Now, you've got some—you had some who were saying, cynically, just claiming the opposite, that somehow this was a bill that institutionalized bailouts. What this bill did was it said, no, if you have a firm on Wall Street that fails, the financial industry is going to pay—not taxpayers. So a vote for reform is a vote to end taxpayer-funded bailouts once and for all. If a crisis like this again happens, financial firms are going to foot the bill. That's point number one.

Point number two—we're going to close the loopholes that allowed derivatives and—all these other large, risky deals that don't make a lot of economic sense and that could threaten our entire economy—we want to bring those deals out into the—out of the dark alleys of our financial system into the light of day, so that everybody knows exactly what's happening, what risks are being taken—investors, shareholders, everybody knows what's going on. That's the second thing.

Protecting and Informing the Public

Number three—this reform is going to give you more power because we're going to put in place the strongest consumer financial protections in history. Because—and the reason this is important—the reason this is important, this crisis wasn't just the result of what happened on Wall Street. It also happened because there were a lot of decisions by folks out on Main Street who were taking out mortgages they didn't understand, credit cards they didn't understand, auto loans that weren't a good deal. Some took on obligations they couldn't afford. But millions of others were deceived or misled by shifting terms and confusing conditions and forests of fine print.

And your attorney general, Lisa Madigan, has been fighting on behalf of consumers in this state [Illinois] and she knows how badly we need these protections. In fact, Lisa and a bunch of other attorney generals came to testify on behalf of the need for these consumer protection bills because they see this stuff in their offices every day. And it's true all across the country.

Now, some argue that giving consumers more information in clear, concise ways is somehow going to stifle competition. I believe the opposite. See, I think if you know what you're buying, you can make a good decision. And that means that the companies, instead of competing to see who can offer the most confusing products, companies will have to compete the old-fashioned way: by offering the best product.

But that's not going to reduce innovation or competition. You just should be knowing what you're buying. It's like a lemon law, right? You don't want to go into the used car lot and get something where they've changed the odometer and put a fresh coat of paint on some old beater and pretend like it's a new car. Well, it's the same thing with financial products. You should know what you're getting.

More Power to Shareholders

All right, so that's the third thing. Finally, we're going to give the people who own these companies, these financial companies—mainly investors and pension holders and shareholders like many of you—we want you to have more say in the way they're run. Because some of these firms, they've got these huge salaries, huge bonuses that create a perverse incentive to encourage people to take reckless risks. But if you own stock in these companies, you need to get some say in how they operate. You'll get to decide how managers are paid and how those firms operate. And that means that we'll actually in-

Senator Chris Dodd Favors Banking Transparency

[The financial reform bill] will ensure that all financial practices are exposed to the sunlight of transparency, so that exotic instruments like hedge funds and derivatives don't lurk in the shadows and businesses can compete on a level playing field.

And, most importantly, it will restore our financial security so that our economy can create jobs and offer middle-class families a chance to build back the wealth they have lost.

Christopher J. Dodd,
Senate Statement on Wall Street Reform,
June 10, 2010.

crease the connection between Main Street and Wall Street. They'll be more accountable to you.

So that's the reform we've put forward. These are the reforms that we're putting forward: Accountability—which means no more bailouts. Closing loopholes—no more trading of things like derivatives in the shadows. Consumer protections—no more deceptive products. A say on pay—so that we give shareholders a more powerful voice. That's what we're trying to do.

Now, I don't think this should be a partisan issue. Everybody—Republicans, and Democrats, and independents—were hurt by this crisis. So everybody should want to fix it. So I'm very pleased that after a few days of delay, it appears an agreement may be at hand to allow this debate to move forward on the Senate floor on this critical issue. I'm very pleased by that.

And I want to work with anyone—Republican or Democrat—who wants to pursue these reforms in good faith. And there can be some legitimate differences on certain issues, but the bottom line is consumers have to be protected. We have to end bailouts. We've got to make sure that these trading practices are out in the open. We've got to make sure that people have a say in terms of how these firms operate so they're more accountable.

Reform Must Come Now

So as long as we're adhering to those clear principles, then I feel okay. What I don't want is a deal made that is written by the financial industry lobbyists. We've had enough of that. We've had enough of that. I want to listen to what they have to say, but I don't [want] them writing the bill. I don't want Democrats and Republicans agreeing to a bill written by them, for them. I want a bill that's written for you, for the American people.

So we're going to see how this debate unfolds. We're going to get this done. And we're going to get it done because you demand it. It's been two years since this crisis, born on Wall Street, slammed into Main Street with its full fury. And while things aren't nearly back to normal out here, they're getting back to normal pretty quick up there. Some in Washington think this debate is moving too fast. They think, well, this is kind of a political game; let's see how this whole thing can play to our advantage in November.

See, that's not how I play. I've been calling for better rules on Wall Street since 2007, before this crisis happened. So I don't think we're moving too fast. I think we've been moving too slow. It's time to get this done. And I don't think you want to see us wait for another year or two years. I don't think you think Washington is moving too fast. I think you want to get this done.

You shouldn't have to wait another day for the protections from some of the practices that got us into this mess. We can't let the recovery that's finally beginning to take hold fall prey to a whole new round of recklessness. If we don't learn the lessons of this crisis, we doom ourselves to repeat it. And I refuse to let that happen. So the time for reform is now.

Editor's Note: President Barack Obama signed the Dodd-Frank Wall Street Reform and Consumer Protection Act into law on July 21, 2010. Measures present in the final bill included the government oversight of derivatives, federal authority to seize large failing financial institutions, and the creation of an independent consumer protection bureau within the Federal Reserve.

> "The [proposed Wall Street reform] measure virtually assures that risky lending practices will continue, with the government backstopping the action."

The Financial Reform Bill Will Lead to More Bailouts

William P. Hoar

In the following viewpoint, William P. Hoar claims that the Barack Obama administration and leading Democratic reformers are demonizing Wall Street banks and proposing regulations that will harm the economy and taxpayers. According to Hoar, current reform projects will simply stifle credit and lending and do nothing to eliminate excessive risk taking. Hoar insists that the worst outcome of this proposed legislation is that average citizens will be forced to fund future bailouts if Wall Street succumbs to another crisis. William P. Hoar is a regular contributor to the New American, *the biweekly magazine of the John Birch Society, a conservative organization that supports limited government.*

William P. Hoar, "Paving the Way for Future Bailouts," *New American*, June 7, 2010. Reprinted with permission.

As you read, consider the following questions:

1. Which two mortgage enterprises does Hoar point out are suspiciously not included in the Dodd reform bill?

2. How did government use the SEC and FDIC to harm investors and taxpayers during the 1930s, in Hoar's view?

3. According to Richard Rahn, as cited in the viewpoint, what will the Dodd reform bill compel the thirty-three largest banks in America to purchase?

ITEM: The April 22 [2010] *Washington Post* reported that President [Barack] Obama was making an "assertive stride into the debate on financial regulatory reform." The president flew to New York "to deliver a stern address to an audience that included prominent financial executives, telling them that greater government oversight is in the best interest of the industry—and the country. 'Unless your business model relies on bilking people, there's little to fear from these new rules,' he said."

ITEM: The Democrats, reported the May 1 [2010] *Los Angeles Times*, "are seizing every opportunity to warn that failure to create more effective financial oversight could bring on a repeat of the economic crisis that has cost millions of ordinary people their homes, jobs and financial security."

For example, Treasury Secretary Timothy Geithner, "who usually discusses controversial issues in only the most careful, often technical terms, dismissed critics in an unusually blunt manner . . . , saying, 'Opponents have tried to convince the American people that these reforms will hurt Main Street or help Wall Street. Those arguments won't work because they aren't true.'"

ITEM: In *Newsweek* for May 10 [2010], Daniel Gross argued for financial reform, in part because "Wall Street opposes calls for change." History, declared the business writer, "has shown

The Treasury Can Bail Out "Significant" Banks

[The financial reform bill] is mainly a cover for unlimited and permanent bailout authority granted to the Treasury Department. Under this legislation the Treasury would be able to make loan guarantees for any institution that is deemed to be "systemically significant," a term that can be open to many interpretations and no doubt will be as things progress. This is similar to the blank check written in the TARP [Troubled Asset Relief Program] legislation during the bailouts of 2008–present, now totaling close to $25 trillion dollars of total cost.

Brandon Turbeville,
"Regulatory Reform Bill: Another Round of Bailouts,"
Infowars.com, April 22, 2010.

that banks often don't know what's good for them. In the 1930s, banks opposed the creation of the SEC [Securities and Exchange Commission] and FDIC [Federal Deposit Insurance Corporation], which laid the groundwork for the industry's remarkable growth over the next 80 years."

CORRECTION: Those resisting the imposition of some 1,400 pages of financial regulatory legislation, one gathers from the sermonizing of the righteous backers of the reforms, are crooks, liars, or ignoramuses. The proponents of onerous and expensive government controls, on the other hand, are all honorable men looking out for our best interests. We know this because they tell us so, repeatedly and in full voice.

Yet, somehow, the observation of [American poet and philosopher Ralph Waldo] Emerson springs to mind: "The louder he talked of his honor, the faster we counted our spoons."

Reform-Minded Hypocrites

And speaking of such honorable men, there's Senator Chris Dodd (D-Conn.), the lead Senator behind financial reform. After a much criticized $50 billion industry-financed liquidation fund was removed from the bill recently, Dodd insisted: "We've ended the 'too big to fail' debate. So no longer do I expect any argument to be made that this bill exposes the American taxpayer."

[This is the] same Senator Dodd who was one of the leading recipients of political contributions from Fannie Mae [Federal National Mortgage Corporation] and Freddie Mac [Federal Home Loan Mortgage Corporation]—the troubled government-sponsored entities under his purview, since nationalized, that were at the heart of the housing bubble. He has been plagued by accounts of sweetheart mortgage loan deals [discounted mortgage Dodd supposedly received from Countrywide Financial]. Less than two months before the government deemed it necessary to start bailing out Fannie and Freddie in 2008, the Honorable Mr. Dodd declared: "To suggest somehow that [Fannie Mae and Freddie Mac] are in trouble is simply not accurate." Such a checkered history and evidence of fatuity might have embarrassed a less honorable man.

Fannie and Freddie are perfect examples of entities given a pass as "too big to fail." Accordingly, taxpayers are being bled white to cover their losses. The Congressional Budget Office estimates that it will cost $389 *billion* to bail them out by 2019. They are *not* covered by the Dodd bill. "Unreformed, they are sure to kill taxpayers again," observes the *Wall Street Journal*. The Obama administration, notes the paper, "won't even put the companies on budget for fear of the deficit impact."

Nor do Dodd's assertions about the taxpayers' supposed lack of exposure square with the facts. Indeed, the measure virtually assures that risky lending practices will continue, with the government backstopping the action; it would also create what critics term "Fannie Mae 2.0." As noted in the Heritage Foundation's *Foundry* blog:

> The problems with the Dodd bill go beyond its failure to let Fannie and Freddie wither into extinction. While Dodd has agreed to get rid of the $50 billion bailout fund, the underlying bailout authority still remains. Now taxpayers are expected to front the government money while firms are liquidated. But the irresponsible creditors who let those firms borrow money irresponsibly would still be eligible for taxpayer bailouts. According to the *Washington Post*, "a failing firm would be forced to pay back the government any money they received above what they would have gotten under a bankruptcy proceeding." But how does the government know what creditors would have gotten if the company went into bankruptcy?

Bureaucrats Should Not Run the Economy

While there are flourishes of misdirection about punishing big firms on behalf of the little people, this is largely lip service for the naïfs. The legislation, as is typical, is being sold under false pretenses. *Newsweek*'s business writer may prefer to pretend otherwise, but bureaucrats really do not know how to run intricate markets better than the markets would if allowed to operate freely. As demonstrated in any number of historical accounts, influential business interests have long colluded *with* government to exclude competitors. During the 1930s, the SEC enforced price-fixing on behalf of Wall Street against the interests of investors, and the creation of the FDIC transferred risks from depositors to taxpayers, a move that eventually cost hundreds of billions of dollars in the savings and loan bailout [in the late 1980s].

Demagoguery still works, however. What the treasury secretary says is one thing, but what he does is something else. As Cato Institute senior fellow Alan Reynolds has noted, the

Obama team has actually made big banks even bigger. Geithner and others, he writes, have spent "the past two years using arm-twisting, sweetheart deals and FDIC guarantees to make sure the biggest banks became much bigger—by taking over failing banks, brokerage houses and mortgage lenders."

Restricting Credit and Dampening Competition

The reform is filled with loopholes and exclusions; it restricts credit and targets real competition. As summarized by Richard Rahn, chairman of the Institute for Global Economic Growth, "The 'Dodd financial reform' bill . . . will make it illegal for 99.6 percent of the population to invest in needed new and promising start-up companies while at the same time ensuring that the 33 largest banks, which control 92 percent of all bank assets, will be required to purchase more federal government debt before giving loans to businesses and individuals. Quite simply, the government is continuing to practice financial fascism."

Even when he was taking some public heat, the head of Goldman Sachs, Lloyd Blankfein, admitted to a Senate subcommittee: "The biggest beneficiary of reform is Wall Street itself." Imagine.

As former Oklahoma representative Ernest Istook [Jr.] explained in the *Daily Caller*:

> Obama claims that so long as taxpayer money doesn't go directly to a company or to its shareholders, it's not a bailout. But he considers it okay to send billions to pay off that company's creditors—who typically are big companies and Wall Street firms. To the rest of us, paying a company's debts IS the bailout, as we've already seen happen multiple times. . . .

> Obama's tough talk against Wall Street draws headlines. But when whipping boy Goldman Sachs says they like the pro-

posed punishment, they're not being masochists. They know that they're getting a government guarantee that they and their friends—as creditors—won't suffer losses when a business partner goes under.

The financial regulatory bill will lead to more harm should it become law. The overall objective doesn't change: privatize profits and socialize risks. When the smoke clears and the mirrors are put away, the true costs would be borne by Main Street and the taxpayers, not the "Wall Street" bogeyman.

Editor's Note: President Barack Obama signed the Dodd-Frank Wall Street Reform and Consumer Protection Act into law on July 21, 2010. Measures present in the final bill included the government oversight of derivatives, federal authority to seize large failing financial institutions, and the creation of an independent consumer protection bureau within the Federal Reserve.

"*A financial system that once thrived on entrepreneurial risk and low barriers to entry for investment will now deny admittance to everyone except those sophisticated enough, connected enough, and flush enough with campaign contributions to do business with government and pay the price of entry.*"

The Financial Reform Bill Will Create Crony Capitalism

Paul Ryan

Wisconsin Republican Paul Ryan is a member of the US House of Representatives. He argues in the following viewpoint that the financial reform bill will create a stronger bond between government and business, inviting big banks that have the capital to continue to influence legislation aimed at regulating their transactions. He maintains that the reform measures will harm only small banks and their patrons because these institutions do not have the money or government connections to navigate the rules and bureaucracy that the bill will impose. For Ryan, this is a

Paul Ryan, "Wall Street 'Reform' Just More Crony Capitalism," realclearpolitics.com, May 20, 2010. Reprinted with permission.

continuation of the crony capitalism that for so long has allowed Wall Street banks to speculate wildly without regulation and that has brought about the current financial crisis.

As you read, consider the following questions:

1. According to Ryan, why has the term "pro-market" tainted Republicans in recent years?

2. How does the proposed reform bill punish small, entry-level ("too-small-to-succeed") financial institutions, according to Ryan?

3. As Ryan reports, what did Senator John McCain propose phasing out from the two government-sponsored enterprises, Freddie Mac and Fannie Mae?

Democrats are nervous. Really nervous. They would like nothing more than to turn the page on their health care takeover, taxpayer-funded bailouts, reckless spending, and exploding debt. In the face of fierce political headwinds, the party running Washington is making an effort to advance its ideology at all costs.

Financial regulatory reform, the thinking goes, provides Democrats an issue where the politics finally align with the Left's policy preferences. Republicans, they believe, can be walked into a convenient political trap by opposing what Democrats call "Wall Street reform." President [Barack] Obama has mastered the art of bank populism, premised on class warfare, by tapping into powerful emotions of envy, anger, and fear.

From an ideological perspective, big government can combine with big business to advance a more progressivist society. For self-described "progressives," the agenda is straightforward: expand government; co-opt big business; direct the capital markets from Washington to pursue "social justice." Think Fannie [Mae (Federal National Mortgage Corporation)] and Freddie [Mac (Federal Home Loan Mortgage Corporation); two government-supported mortgage enterprises] by much higher orders of magnitude.

Mistakenly Abetting Industry at the Expense of Competition

Over the past decade, the thinking has been much less clear for conservatives. Being "pro-market" has been fundamentally confused with "pro-business." Conservatives who came to Congress to defend and promote free enterprise have often been led to believe that pathway lies in bolstering established firms as they navigate the maze of government regulations and taxes. These instincts are correct, but the implementation is often flawed. All too often, the results of these efforts have been to exacerbate crony capitalism [where business success is determined by political connections]—erecting barriers to entry against potential competitors to firms that are currently on top.

For their part, companies seeking such protection have a right to pursue their narrow self-interest; but when these actions involve reducing open competition and transparency for short-term gain, they do so to the detriment of the very free enterprise system that made their success possible.

Republicans, who profess their zeal for democratic capitalism as the greatest source of human flourishing, all too often have aided the "kings of industry" in pulling the drawbridge up after they've taken the castle. Conservatives must recover the fundamentals of what is needed to defend the free enterprise system. We can begin by rejecting the current financial regulatory overhaul moving through Congress, and by offering alternatives that apply the essential principles that form a true free enterprise system.

Creating a New Bureaucracy Where Crony Capitalism Will Flourish

The financial regulatory overhaul is not reform. Its fundamental architecture expands and centralizes power in Washington, doubling down on the root causes of the 2008 crisis. It is based on a vision that government can foresee future crises and avert them, despite the fact that an army of regulators never saw the most recent crisis coming.

The complex array of new councils, agencies, and bureaucracies creates endless channels for crony capitalists to penetrate. A financial system that once thrived on entrepreneurial risk and low barriers to entry for investment will now deny admittance to everyone except those sophisticated enough, connected enough, and flush enough with campaign contributions to do business with government and pay the price of entry.

Institutions deemed "too-small-to-succeed" would not be afforded the explicit protections given to the largest firms, resulting in higher borrowing costs and higher hurdles to succeed relative to their well-connected competitors. Unprecedented authority over the operations of financial institutions would be vested in the Federal Deposit Insurance Corporation (FDIC). The FDIC would be authorized to seize risky financial institutions if a council of regulators, chaired by the Treasury Secretary, believes a company is in danger of default and poses systemic risk. Once a company has been seized, the FDIC oversees its entire resolution process, including restructuring the order of creditor obligations—serving as creditor, manager, and referee.

Conflicts of interest will inevitably arise on how to treat creditors of failed firms, and increasingly, what were once economic decisions will now be political decisions. Dispelling the market discipline of our profit-and-*loss* free enterprise system, collusion between government bureaucrats and their private-sector counterparts will determine winners and losers.

Alternatives to the Government Approach

Despite roughly 1400 pages of text in the legislation, the destructive role of the government-backed housing giants remains a glaring omission. Enabled by Congress, Fannie Mae and Freddie Mac wrought havoc on the housing market and remain on operational life support as taxpayers subsidize their failure. After their leading role in the subprime mortgage crisis, they've received $145 billion in taxpayer dollars, with no limit to additional funding. Fannie and Freddie demonstrate just how big federally blessed and guaranteed businesses can grow—and just how hard they can fall.

A number of key corrections to mitigate crony capitalism's destruction have been rejected throughout the Senate debate. Senator John McCain, for example, offered an amendment to end the privatized profit/socialized loss model of Fannie and Freddie, phasing out costly taxpayer subsidies. House Republicans have also put forth serious reforms for Fannie and Freddie, as part of our larger financial reform alternative—despite being shut out of the process in House.

There is no shortage of innovative alternatives to the heavy-handed government approach making its way through Congress—alternatives that make the distinction between "pro-market" and "pro-business." Although a bold departure from the status quo, a proposal put forth by Boston University economist Laurence Kotlikoff calls for banks to stick to their fundamental purpose of financial intermediation rather than taking on the excessive risks with no strings attached that have led to taxpayer-funded bailouts. Real reform must decouple America's economic well-being from the fate of a select few financial firms.

Another approach, one that works within the current financial framework, has been offered by Oliver Hart of Harvard University and Luigi Zingales of the University of Chicago. Their proposal addresses the "too-big-to-fail" question through the use of a market-based trigger that tells firms when to beef up capital. This approach is aimed to better balance "the need to curb reckless risk taking . . . while making sure not to unduly constrain economic activity, investment and growth."

Good Faith Reform Should Break Government Control over Business

Failure to reform the system poses clear risks, but the frenzied push to score a legislative victory prior to the November [2010] midterms with a deeply flawed bill poses greater risk. A good-faith reform effort should not continue indefinitely, but the Financial Crisis Inquiry Commission, for example, has been essentially cast aside by the very same Congress that tasked the commission to investigate the crisis and issue its report later this year. The Democratic leaders on both ends of Pennsylvania Avenue have opted to rush a bill into law,[1] putting ideological goals and campaign strategy ahead of underlying catalysts for real reform.

The federal government has a critical role in helping ensure financial markets are fair and transparent, and holding accountable those that violate the rules. Reform should aim to restore the principles that have made credit available to American families and entrepreneurs and our capital markets the envy of the world: freedom to participate, an unbreakable link between performance and reward, continued attachment to risk, and a sense of responsibility that ensures those who seek to reap the gains also bear the full risks of losses.

For millions of American families, the real pain from the past financial crisis can still be felt. The financial services sector needs reform—yet the overhaul before Congress exacerbates the worst aspects of today's system. Washington is attempting to solve every problem with greater government control, and higher spending, taxes, and record levels of debt—breathing new life into crony capitalism across our economy.

---

1. President Barack Obama signed the Dodd-Frank Wall Street Reform and Consumer Protection Act into law on July 21, 2010.

> *"Unfortunately, the proposal for regulatory reform now before the Senate does not eliminate the concept of too-big-to-fail."*

The Financial Reform Bill Needs to Ensure That No Bank Is "Too Big to Fail"

Thomas Hoenig

In the following viewpoint, Thomas Hoenig claims that the financial reform bill operates on the assumption that some banks are "too big to fail" and are worth bailing out with taxpayer money when crises occur. Hoenig insists that this persistent belief has undermined fair competition between little banks and big banks because creditors will opt to stay with big banks, knowing that their funds will be bailed out in emergencies. Hoenig, the president and chief executive officer of the Federal Reserve Bank of Kansas City and the senior member of the Federal Reserve System's Federal Open Market Committee, also takes issue with proposed rules that change the purview of the Federal Reserve to cover only the largest banks, leaving little banks under the watchful eye of the Federal Deposit Insurance Corporation (FDIC). In Hoenig's opinion, this not only ties the Federal Reserve to these

Thomas Hoenig, "Keep the Fed on Main Street," *New York Times*, April 18, 2010. www.nytimes.com. Reproduced by permission.

large institutions, but also deprives the Federal Reserve from its appointed role of overseeing and protecting banks across America. The final version of the financial reform bill did not transfer banking oversight to the FDIC and gave the Federal Reserve new powers to regulate non-bank financial institutions.

As you read, consider the following questions:

1. According to Hoenig, what has happened to the size of big banks' assets as a result of the dampening of competition with little banks?

2. As Hoenig reports, what entity would need to petition a special panel of US Bankruptcy Court judges to begin transitioning a failing financial firm into receivership?

3. Why does the author reject the receivership mandates of the proposed reform bill?

Last week [in early April 2010], I visited Santa Fe, N.M., and spoke to one of America's many Main Streets: more than 300 small-business owners, real estate developers, artists, bankers and other citizens. A good number of them, experiencing the fallout of the financial crisis and feeling the stress it put on New Mexico's banks, were angry and frustrated.

You see, New Mexico's financial institutions were not too big to fail. They were never invited to meetings and told to accept financing from the Troubled Asset Relief Program [that bailed out banks]. As a result, banks and residents of Santa Fe, like those in towns all over Middle America, have struggled mightily through this recession. It was clear that, like politics, the effects of financial crises are mostly local.

This explains why it undermines the very foundation of our economic system when the government decides that a financial institution is too big or too powerful to fail. The big banks and investment companies hold a significant advantage in the competition for funds (for example, from depositors and bond holders), because creditors know that they will be bailed out when a crisis occurs. This advantage has systematically undermined the competitive position of every smaller bank, and has enabled the largest banking organizations to more than double their share of industry assets since the 1990s. These trends serve neither the national economy nor communities like Santa Fe. And in the end, they are a burden on taxpayers.

Special Considerations for Big Banks

Unfortunately, the proposal for regulatory reform now before the Senate[1] does not eliminate the concept of too-big-to-fail, and it deliberately narrows the central bank's focus to Wall Street alone. This undermines reform in at least two important ways.

First, the decision to close a large financial firm that is failing would depend on the Treasury Department's petitioning a panel of three United States Bankruptcy Court judges for approval to place the firm in receivership with the Federal Deposit Insurance Corporation. The panel would have 24 hours to make a decision, and if it turned down the petition, the Treasury could re-file and subsequent appeals could be considered. So a decision to put the firm in receivership might not be timely enough under the circumstances. And experience tells us that the urgency of the moment would likely motivate politically sensitive officials to simply pursue a bailout.

Instead, the new law should require that any institution deemed insolvent, based on an established, objective set of criteria, be placed into receivership and resolved in an orderly fashion—just as banks on Main Street are.

1. President Barack Obama signed the Dodd-Frank Wall Street Reform and Consumer Protection Act into law on July 21, 2010. Measures present in the final bill included the government oversight of derivatives, federal authority to seize large failing financial institutions, and the creation of a consumer protection bureau within the Federal Reserve.

The CEO of the Federal Reserve Bank of New York Claims Too-Big-to-Fail Banks Are a Moral Hazard

Having some firms that are too big to fail creates moral hazard. These firms are able to obtain funding on more attractive terms because debt holders expect that the government will intervene rather than allow failure. In addition, too big to fail creates perverse incentives. In a too-big-to-fail regime, firms have an incentive to get large, not because it facilitates greater efficiency, but instead because the implicit government backstop enables the too-big-to-fail firm to achieve lower funding costs.

William C. Dudley,
"The U.S. Financial System: Where We Have Been,
Where We Are and Where We Need to Go,"
Remarks at the Reserve Bank of Australia's
50th Anniversary Symposium,
February 8, 2010. www.newyorkfed.org.

Limiting the Role of the Federal Reserve

Second, the proposed financial reform legislation would significantly narrow the supervisory role of the Federal Reserve [the Fed], so that it would oversee only the very largest institutions, most of which are headquartered in New York City. Congress established the Federal Reserve System in 1913 with 12 banks in a federated structure, like our political system, so that it would include regional perspectives to counterbalance the influence of Wall Street and Washington. To now narrow the Fed's supervision to just the largest banks would be to devalue those broader perspectives. The Federal Reserve would no longer be the central bank of the United States, but only the central bank of Wall Street.

The flawed logic of this proposed change is that only the biggest firms are systemically important; that only they require the contingency lending that the Fed provides at its discount window; that only they will be involved in future crises; and that overseeing these firms is sufficient to provide the "macro-prudential supervision" the central bank's charter requires. By this reasoning, the 6,700 other banks and the communities they serve are of no immediate consequence to the mission of the Federal Reserve.

The Federal Reserve Needs to Help Main Street as Well as Wall Street

Who outside of Wall Street can legitimately support such thinking? As a commissioned examiner and head of supervision in the Fed's Kansas City district in the 1980s, I am a veteran of financial crises involving energy, real estate and agriculture in the Midwest and West. I can say with confidence that a regional financial crisis and its accompanying loss of jobs is just as harmful as the current Wall Street crisis has been for communities like Santa Fe.

Because the Federal Reserve supervises banks and bank holding companies of all sizes, it is able to address regional as well as national banking problems when they erupt. In addition, I and other Fed presidents can take information about regional financial and economic conditions into monetary policy discussions.

Without the Fed seeing the view from every corner of America, without every bank knowing it will be treated the same, the Federal Reserve cannot do its job and direct the same attention to the smallest firms as the largest. It cannot serve Main Street.

> "If we want to 'lock in' bank trust-busting, or require the government to turn to conservatorships before it turns to bailouts, then we will want that legislation immediately. But I don't think we need it to begin reforming banking now."

Legislation Already Exists Concerning "Too Big to Fail"

David Zaring

David Zaring is an assistant professor of legal studies at the University of Pennsylvania's Wharton School of Business. In the following viewpoint, he claims that Congress should not be putting so much attention into passing legislation that would ensure that none of the large financial institutions are "too big to fail." In Zaring's opinion, existing antitrust laws could easily be amended to break up big banks' dominance of market shares and the Federal Reserve and Federal Deposit Insurance Corporation already have powers to take failing banks into conservatorship. Zaring contends that fixing or tweaking these laws can be done without congressional mandate. Finally, Zaring notes that legislation might be wrongheaded if its intent is simply to carve

David Zaring, "Why Congress Should Not Fix 'Too Big to Fail,'" *Washington Post*, April 23, 2009. Reproduced by permission.

up banks just because of their size. He maintains that size does not necessarily mean these institutions are unhealthy.

As you read, consider the following questions:

1. Who does Zaring say would be responsible for revising antitrust statutes to make them apply to the current banking crisis?

2. As Zaring asserts, who has always had the power to mandate minimum capital requirements upon banks to hedge against failure?

3. In Zaring's view, how might the public rethink the phrase "too big to fail" so that it would not only imply more government bailouts?

At the hearing earlier this week [of April 19–25, 2009] before the Joint Economic Committee [JEC] nobody liked banks that were "too big to fail." [CEO of the Federal Reserve Bank of Kansas City] Thomas Hoenig decried the "financial megamergers" that led to the problem in the first place. [Former chief economist of the International Monetary Fund] Simon Johnson regretted that "[f]inance became big relative to the economy, largely because of . . . political decisions" deregulating the banks that should be revisited.

[Economist and Columbia University professor] Joseph Stiglitz said that "[t]here are but two solutions: breaking up the institutions or regulating them heavily. For reasons that I will make clear, we need to do both." Johnson and Hoenig agreed.

No Legislation Needed

What can we do about oversized banks? And are they really so bad?

I'll consider the solutions first, and then briefly look at the problem. Johnson proposes solving 'Too Big to Fail' through trust-busting. Hoenig suggests conservatorships like the one the Federal Deposit Insurance Corp. [FDIC] imposed on [bank and trust company] Continental Illinois. I will add leverage caps to the mix, as the G20 [organization of 20 central bank governors and national finance ministers in the industrialized world] suggested that it would support a multinational approach along those lines.

In my view, none of these strategies to shrink the banks requires legislation from Congress, although both Hoenig and Johnson encourage the modernization of those laws. If you think that banks play an outsized role in the political process, or if you think that banking reform legislation will take years to complete, you should be glad to hear this.

It's true that the principal antitrust laws have not been amended in over a century. But that is because antitrust law is a flexible, judge- and prosecutor-made doctrine. In the 1980s, the Department of Justice decided to take a much more hands-off approach to large market share. That decision survived the [Ronald] Reagan administration, and it has been quite popular with economists (and even more popular with law professors).

Emend Existing Powers

But there is no reason it could not be revisited now. And if the Justice Department wants to focus its attention on banks instead of, say, health care providers, the beauty of those old, broad statutes is that they can be easily interpreted to permit that new enforcement choice.

And the murky powers of conservatorship that the FDIC and Federal Reserve have long had were, if anything, clarified and increased with the 1991 passage of legislation in the aftermath of the S&L [savings and loan] crisis. That gave the FDIC and Fed "prompt corrective action" powers to impose conservatorships quickly.

Finally, federal banking regulators have always had the power to devise minimum capital requirements for banks (say, by keeping 8.5 percent of your capital in cash on hand); leverage caps work essentially the same way.

These regulatory fixes are "stroke of a pen" fixes. We might still want a congressional endorsement of them, at least eventually. And if we want to "lock in" bank trust-busting, or require the government to turn to conservatorships before it turns to bailouts, then we will want that legislation immediately. But I don't think we need it to begin reforming banking now.

But should we reform banking now? Is too big to fail really so bad? Given the regularity of financial panics, I think it probably is. One cautionary note, however. 'Too Big to Fail' doesn't have to stand for an implicit government guarantee. It could stand for a sensible strategy of scope, economies of scale, and diversification. Investors often want companies to do those things. German, Swiss and Japanese banks grew very big partly, I suspect, because their regulators concluded that their size and sophistication meant that they really couldn't fail. Those banks are still very big (some of the German and Swiss banks might even be healthy), suggesting that many still appear to believe, unlike the witnesses at the JEC hearing, that size can equal strength.

> "I agree that regulated, transparent swap activity is a necessary part of our economy—it just has no place inside of a bank where too many innocent bystanders are put at risk."

The Financial Reform Bill Should Force High-Risk Derivatives Trading Out of Banks

Blanche Lincoln

Blanche Lincoln is a US Senator from Arkansas and the chair of the Senate Agriculture Committee. In April 2010, she and fellow Democratic Senator Chris Dodd of Connecticut merged two separate reform measures into one bill that sought to sever the trading of derivatives from banking institutions and to compel that these trades went through clearinghouses to reduce systemic risk if these trades failed. The main concept was to force big banks to conduct these risky ventures at their own hazard, barring them from using federal money to cover losses if markets collapsed. In the following viewpoint, a statement made before the US Senate, Senator Lincoln explains why she believes volatile

Blanche Lincoln, "Statement to the Senate on S. 3217: The Restoring American Financial Stability Act of 2010," lincoln.senate.gov, May 5, 2010. Reprinted by permission.

derivatives—contracts based on expected future prices of commodities, interest rates, or other financial indices—should not be part of taxpayer-backed institutions. In her view, banks should spin off their swap desks and manage them as separate entities not tied to federally insured banking practices such as loans, mortgages, and deposits. She argues that if these trades remain in-house, taxpayers will end up footing the bill for future market failures driven by these unstable contracts.

As you read, consider the following questions:

1. As Lincoln reports, how many banking institutions are currently responsible for 97 percent of swap activity?

2. Why is Senator Lincoln distressed by skyrocketing FDIC insurance premiums for small banks across the country?

3. By moving swaps from banks to ancillary institutions, Lincoln acknowledges that these trades will no longer be overseen by the FDIC. What agencies, however, does she say would continue to monitor such trades?

As Chairman of the Senate Agriculture Committee, I am proud to have included this provision [on derivatives] in Wall Street reform legislation approved on a bipartisan vote by our committee two weeks ago [in April 2010]. I am also proud that it is included in the Dodd-Lincoln legislation that we are considering today.

This provision seeks to ensure that banks get back to the business of banking. Under our current system, there are a handful of big banks that are simply no longer acting like banks. Surely every member of this body is aware that the operation of risky swaps activities was the spark that lit the flame that very nearly destroyed our economy.

In my view, banks were never intended to perform these activities, which have been the single largest factor to these institutions growing so large that taxpayers had no choice but to bail them out in order to prevent total economic ruin.

Separating Risky Swaps
from Banking Activity

My provision seeks to accomplish two goals: first, getting banks back to performing the duties they were meant to perform—taking deposits and making loans for mortgages, small businesses and commercial enterprise; and second, separating out the activities that put these institutions in peril.

This provision makes clear that engaging in risky derivative dealing [making financial agreements based on expected future assets] is not central to the business of banking. Under Section 716 [the derivatives title], the Federal Reserve and FDIC [Federal Deposit Insurance Corporation] will be prohibited from providing any federal assistance and funds to bail out swap dealers and major swap participants.

Currently, five of the largest commercial banks account for 97 percent of the commercial bank notional swap activity. That is a huge concentration of economic power, which is why I am in no way surprised that several individuals are seeking to remove it from the bill.

This provision will ensure that our community banks on Main Street won't pay the price for reckless behavior on Wall Street. Community banks are the backbone of economic activity for cities and towns throughout the country. They don't deal in risky swaps that put the whole financial system in jeopardy. Instead they perform the day-to-day business of banking—making the smart, conservative decisions that banking institutions should be making.

Unfortunately, Mr. President, we saw the five largest banks begin to fail in part because of risky swaps activity—activity that should never have been part of their operation in the first place. Sadly, it was our community bankers and their depositors who were left footing the bill.

Community banks were forced to pay for a problem they did not create. Mr. President, small banks are still paying the price. In 2009, we saw 140 bank failures and now the costs of

FDIC insurance premiums are skyrocketing for community banks. Higher insurance rates mean less lending.

Less lending means that now individuals and small businesses are also paying the price. The FDIC reported that in 2009 the bank industry reduced lending by 7.4 percent, the biggest decrease since 1942.

I am a strong believer that you build an economic recovery from the ground up and if small and medium-sized businesses aren't getting the capital they need to grow their businesses, something is wrong. The economy simply will not recover unless we free up lending.

Spreading Misinformation and Falsehoods

Unfortunately, Wall Street lobbyists are doing everything they can to distort this provision—spreading misinformation and untruths.

Mr. President, the suggestion that this provision will force derivatives into the dark without oversight, is absolutely false. The Dodd-Lincoln bill makes it abundantly clear that all swaps activity will be vigorously regulated by the Fed [Federal Reserve], the Commodity Futures Trading Commission [CFTC] and the Securities Exchange Commission.

My good friend from New Hampshire, Senator [Judd] Gregg, my friend from Tennessee, Senator [Bob] Corker, Wall Street lobbyists, and others in recent days have somehow argued that by pushing out risky swaps from the nation's largest banks, like JPMorgan [Chase], Bank of America, Wells Fargo, Goldman Sachs or Citigroup, that somehow swaps will no longer be regulated.

This is just plain wrong.

Just because these swaps desks will no longer be overseen by the FDIC does not mean that they will not be subject to the bill's strong regulation by the market regulators—the SEC and CFTC. In short, they simply ignore the strong provisions

---

Section 716 of Lincoln's Bill Will Shrink the Market Dominance of Big Banks

By requiring that dealing and trading derivatives move to separately capitalized affiliates that do not have access to Fed [Federal Reserve] lending facilities or FDIC [Federal Deposit Insurance Corporation] guarantees, section 716 will also contribute to shrinking the size of individual institutions' positions and the market itself. The huge capital reserves of the five institutions that dominate the U.S. market will no longer be available to support their outsized positions.

Jane D'Arista,
"Why Section 716 Is the Indispensable Reform,"
The Baseline Scenario, *June 10, 2010.*
http://baselinescenario.com.

---

included in the rest of the underlying bill. Convenient for their argument, but not so convenient when seeking the truth.

Let me reiterate—every swaps dealer and major swap participant will be subject to strong regulation.

Wall Street lobbyists have also argued that this will prevent banks from using swaps to hedge their risks. Again, completely false.

Banks who have been acting as banks will be able to continue doing business as they always have. Community banks using swaps to hedge their interest rate risk on their loan portfolio will continue to be able to do so and, most importantly, we want them to do so. Community banks offering a swap in connection with a loan to a commercial customer are also still in the business of banking and will not be impacted.

Using these products to manage risk and designing exotic swaps—which have led to the financial demise of places like Jefferson County, Alabama, Orange County, California, and the country of Greece—are two very different things. Hopefully, this is something my colleagues will understand.

Mr. President, Wall Street lobbyists have also said this provision will move $300 trillion worth of swap activities outside of the banks. My question is, why is this activity there in the first place?

I agree that regulated, transparent swap activity is a necessary part of our economy—it just has no place inside of a bank where too many innocent bystanders are put at risk.

Broad Support for the Dodd-Lincoln Bill

Mr. President, despite what those on Wall Street may be saying, this provision is an important part of real Wall Street reform. It has broad support from the Independent Community Bankers of America, the Consumer Federation of America, AARP [an advocacy group for older Americans], labor unions, and leading economists like Nobel Prize–winning Joseph Stiglitz, among others.

Let me read what these groups and individuals are saying about this provision.

Americans for Financial Reform which includes groups such as the AFL-CIO [American Federation of Labor—Congress of Industrial Organizations], NAACP [National Association for the Advancement of Colored People], Consumers Union writes—

> The over 250 consumer, employee, investor, community and civil rights groups who are members of Americans for Financial Reform (AFR) write to express strong support for Section 716 ("Prohibition Against Federal Government Bailouts of Swaps Entities") as part of the Dodd-Lincoln substitute to the Restoring [American] Financial Stability Act of 2010.

It is now almost universally recognized that the fuse that lit the worldwide economic meltdown in the fall of 2008 was the $600 trillion, severely under-capitalized and unregulated and opaque swaps market, dominated by the world's largest banks. Section 716 is designed to ensure that the American taxpayer is not the banker of last resort, as was true in the bank bailouts in 2008–2009, for casino-like investments marketed by large Wall Street swap dealer-banks. Section 716 is a flat ban on federal government assistance to "any swap entity," especially in instances where that entity cannot fulfill obligations emanating from highly risky swaps transactions.

Section 716 will require the five largest swaps dealer banks to sever their swaps desks from the bank holding corporate structure. Those five banks are: Goldman Sachs, Morgan Stanley, JPMorgan Chase, Citigroup, and Bank of America, the institutions involved in well over 90 percent of swaps transactions. Under Section 716 a "swap entity" and a banking entity could not be contained within the same bank holding company, if the bank holding company has access to federal assistance.

By quarantining highly risky swaps trading from banking altogether, federally insured deposits will not be put at risk by toxic swaps transactions. Moreover, banks will be forced to behave like banks, focusing on extending credit in a manner that builds economic strength as opposed to fostering worldwide economic instability. Finally, the spun-off swaps entity will be sufficiently isolated to permit the kind of careful prudential oversight mandated by Title VII of the Act as a whole. Title VII ensures that the spun-off entities will both be regulated as institutions under the most rigorous prudential standards, and that almost all of the swaps instruments will be subject to standards for capital adequacy, full transparency, anti-fraud and anti-manipulation.

Nobel Prize–winning economist and former chairman of the Council of Economic Advisers during the [Bill] Clinton administration Joseph Stiglitz writes

> One provision holds particular promise—and has the banks especially riled up. This is the idea that the government should not be responsible for the "counterparty risk"—the risk that a derivatives contract not be fulfilled. It was AIG's inability to fulfill its obligations that led the U.S. government to step into the breach, to the tune of some $182 billion.
>
> The modest proposal of the agriculture committee is that the U.S. government (the Federal Deposit Insurance Corporation) stops underwriting these risks. If banks wish to write derivatives, they would have to do so through a separate affiliate within the holding company. And if the bank made bad gambles, the taxpayer wouldn't have to pick up the tab.
>
> This change would help fix the current system, where those who buy this so-called "insurance" enjoy the subsidy of the essential, free government guarantee; and where competition among the few issuers of these risky products is sufficiently weak that they enjoy high profits.
>
> The Federal Reserve and the Treasury seem to object to the agriculture committee's proposals. These objections show once again the extent to which the Fed and the Treasury have been captured by the institutions that they are supposed to regulate, and reemphasize the need for deeper governance reforms of the Fed than those on the table.
>
> To be sure, banks' high profits from derivatives would help with recapitalization, offsetting the losses they incurred from the risky gambles of the past. But that doesn't mean that the policy of allowing banks to issue derivatives—and laying the risk of failure onto the taxpayer—is right.
>
> Bank recapitalization should be done in an open and transparent way, consistent with sound economic principles.

The Independent Community Bankers of America [ICBA] writes

> ICBA strongly supports Section 106 of the derivatives bill. This section prohibits federal assistance, including federal deposit insurance and access to the Fed's discount window, to swaps entities in connection with their trading in swaps or securities-based swaps.
>
> Main Street and community banks have suffered the brunt of the financial crisis, a crisis caused by Wall Street players and not community banks. Assessments to replenish the Deposit Insurance Fund have increased dramatically for community banks. Large financial players have received hundreds of billions in financial assistance while community banks have been allowed to fail.
>
> Section 106 of Senator Lincoln's derivatives legislation would be an important provision to help ensure that taxpayers and community banks are not on the chopping block should another financial crisis occur. We strongly urge retention of this provision during markup this week. Thank you for keeping the views of community banks in mind.

Mr. President, I ask Unanimous Consent that these letters from Americans for Financial Reform, Professor Stiglitz and the Independent Community Bankers be entered into the Record.

I look forward to working with my colleagues to ensure this legislation remains strong and new loopholes are not created on behalf of Wall Street.

Editor's Note: President Barack Obama signed the Dodd-Frank Wall Street Reform and Consumer Protection Act into law on July 21, 2010. The bill included a modified version of Lincoln's derivatives proposal that allowed banks to participate in derivatives trading, though to a lesser extent.

"If all derivatives market-making activities were moved outside of bank holding companies, most of the activity would no doubt continue, but in less regulated and more highly leveraged venues."

The Financial Reform Bill Should Not Force High-Risk Derivatives Trading Out of Banks

Sheila C. Bair

Sheila C. Bair is the current chairperson of the Federal Deposit Insurance Corporation. In the following viewpoint—a letter to Senators Chris Dodd and Blanche Lincoln—Bair criticizes part of the financial reform bill drafted by the two senators that calls for the separation of risky derivatives trading from the holding companies of banks. Dodd and Lincoln argue that big banks traded wildly in these derivatives—contracts based on expected future prices of commodities, interest rates, or other financial indices—and helped bring about the financial crisis when many of these contracts folded. Bair, on the other hand, contends that

Sheila C. Bair, Sheila Bair Letter to Dodd and Lincoln Re: Derivative Regulations, www.ritholtz.com., April 30, 2010. Reprinted with permission.

some derivatives are already regulated and others would be handily supervised by new regulations calling for the establishment of clearinghouses. She believes if banks are forced to oust their derivatives trading, they will not be able to spread their risks, and any spun-off derivatives trading would end up in unregulated shadow banking services where untold damage would result from future market failures.

As you read, consider the following questions:

1. According to Bair, what is the notional value (face value) of derivatives that would be moved outside insured banks if the Dodd-Lincoln derivatives proposal became law?

2. What activities does Bair agree have no place in banks or bank holding companies?

3. According to Bair, why did FDIC insured banks weather the financial crisis better than other financial institutions?

Dear Chairman [Chris] Dodd and Chairman [Blanche] Lincoln:

Thank you for reaching out to the Federal Deposit Insurance Corporation [FDIC] for our views on Title VII of the "Wall Street Transparency and Accountability Act" contained in S. 3217, the "Restoring American Financial Stability Act of 2010." At the outset, I would like to express my strong support for enhanced regulation of "over-the-counter" (OTC) derivatives and the provisions of the bill which would require centralized clearing and exchange trading of standardized products. If this requirement is applied rigorously it will mean that most OTC contracts will be centrally cleared, a desirable improvement from the bilateral clearing processes used now. I would also like to express my wholehearted endorsement of the ultimate intent of the bill, to protect the deposit insurance fund from high-risk behavior.

Allowing Banks to Keep Derivative Trading In-House

I would like to share some concerns with respect to section 716 of S. 3217, which would require most derivatives activities [financial arrangements based on expected future assets] to be conducted outside of banks and bank holding companies. If enacted, this provision would require that some $294 trillion in notional amount of derivatives be moved outside of banks or from bank holding companies that own insured depository institutions, presumably to nonbank financial firms such as hedge funds and futures commission merchants, or to foreign banking organizations beyond the reach of federal regulation. I would note that credit derivatives—the riskiest—held by banks and bank holding companies (when measured by notional amount) total $25.5 trillion, or slightly less than nine percent of the total derivatives held by these entities.

At the same time, it needs to be pointed out that the vast majority of banks that use OTC derivatives confine their activity to hedging interest rate risk with straightforward interest rate derivatives. Given the continuing uncertainty surrounding future movements in interest rates and the detrimental effects that these could have on unhedged banks, I encourage you to adopt an approach that would allow banks to easily hedge with OTC derivatives. Moreover, I believe that directing standardized OTC products toward exchanges or other central clearing facilities would accomplish the stabilization of the OTC market that we seek to enhance, and would still allow banks to continue the important market-making functions that they currently perform.

Important Risk Management Tools

In addition, I urge you to carefully consider the underlying premise of this provision—that the best way to protect the deposit insurance fund is to push higher risk activities into the so-called shadow sector. To be sure, there are certain activities,

Some Objections to Ousting Derivatives Trading

The derivatives legislation [in the proposed reform bill] would effectively force U.S. banks out of the swaps market. The effect of the prohibition seems not to have been truly considered by Congress and so it seems worthwhile to raise some of the likely consequences of such a prohibition.

As a starting matter, the banks will have to fire people involved in the swaps business and sell assets related to the swaps business. Who will hire the people? Who will buy the assets?

Banks use derivatives for a variety of risk management purposes. For example, when a bank makes a loan to a corporation, it may also enter into a credit default swap that hedges the risk of the loan.

If banks cannot enter into credit default swaps, then they would likely make fewer loans and face greater risk on those loans they did make.

Cadwalader, Wickersham & Taft LLP,
"Some Concerns with the Derivatives Legislation,"
Clients & Friends Memo, May 3, 2010. www.cadwalader.com.

such as speculative derivatives trading, that should have no place in banks or bank holding companies. We believe the Volcker Rule addresses that issue and indeed would be happy to work with you on a total ban on speculative trading, at least in the CDS [credit default swaps] market[1]. At the same

1. The Volcker Rule, named after Federal Reserve chairman Paul Volcker, calls for banks to refrain from credit default swaps and other derivatives trading if these transactions are not performed on behalf of the bank's customers. A version of the rule is part of the final congressional bill.

time, other types of derivatives such as customized interest rate swaps and even some CDS do have legitimate and important functions as risk management tools, and insured banks play an essential role in providing market-making functions for these products.

Banks are not perfect, but we do believe that insured banks as a whole performed better during this crisis because they are subject to higher capital requirements in both the amount and quality of capital. Insured banks also are subject to ongoing prudential supervision by their primary banking regulators, as well as a second pair of eyes through the FDIC's backup supervisory role, which we are strengthening as a lesson of the crisis. If all derivatives market-making activities were moved outside of bank holding companies, most of the activity would no doubt continue, but in less regulated and more highly leveraged venues [i.e., where less capital is needed to buy a derivative]. Even pushing the activity into a bank holding company affiliate would reduce the amount and quality of capital required to be held against this activity. It would also be beyond the scrutiny of the FDIC because we do not have the same comprehensive backup authority over the affiliates of banks as we do with the banks themselves. Such affiliates would have to rely on less stable sources of liquidity, which—as we saw during the past crisis—would be destabilizing to the banking organization in times of financial distress, which in turn would put additional pressure on the insured bank to provide stability. By concentrating the activity in an affiliate of the insured bank, we could end up with less and lower quality capital, less information and oversight for the FDIC, and potentially less support for the insured bank in a time of crisis. Thus, one unintended outcome of this provision would be weakened, not strengthened, protection of the insured bank and the Deposit Insurance Fund, which I know is not the result any of us want.

Keeping the Goal of Stability in Mind

A central lesson of this crisis is that it is difficult to insulate insured banks from risk taking conducted by their nonbanking affiliated entities. When the crisis hit, the shadow sector collapsed, leaving insured banks as the only source of stability. Far from serving as a source of strength, bank holding companies and their affiliates had to draw stability from their insured deposit franchises. We must be careful not to reduce even further the availability of support to insured banks from their holding companies. As a result, we believe policies going forward should recognize the damage regulatory arbitrage caused our economy and craft policies that focus on the quality and strength of regulation as opposed to the business model used to support it.

The FDIC is pleased to continue working with you on this important issue to assure that the final outcome serves all of our goals for a safer and more stable financial sector. We hope that a compromise can be achieved by perhaps moving some derivatives activity into affiliates, so long as capital standards remain as strict as they are for insured depositories and banks continue to be able to fully utilize derivatives for appropriate hedging activities.

Editor's Note: President Barack Obama signed the Dodd-Frank Wall Street Reform and Consumer Protection Act into law on July 21, 2010. The bill included a modified version of the Dodd-Lincoln derivatives proposal that allowed banks to continue participating in derivatives trading, though to a lesser extent.

"While the bill claims to crack down on excesses on Wall Street, its harshest impact will likely be on Main Street businesses that had nothing to do with the crisis."

The Financial Reform Bill Is So Gutted That It Will Change Nothing

John Berlau

In the following viewpoint, John Berlau claims that the Dodd-Frank financial reform bill puts mandates on every business and enterprise except for the ones that were at the root of the financial crisis. In Berlau's opinion, the bill is counterproductive and possibly unconstitutional. The bill allows the Federal Reserve and Treasury Department to seize firms that are not asking for a bailout. Essentially, the bill does nothing to ensure the prevention of another financial crisis. John Berlau is director of the Center for Investors and Entrepreneurs at the Competitive Enterprise Institute and author of the book Eco-Freaks: Environmentalism Is Hazardous to Your Health!*.*

John Berlau, "Dodd-Frank Finance Bill Underscores Big US Intervention," *Newsmax*, July 15, 2010. Reproduced by permission.

As you read, consider the following questions:

1. According to the article, what government-sponsored enterprises are untouched by the Dodd-Frank financial regulation bill?

2. What will the financial regulation bill's "orderly liquidation" authority allow?

3. As stated in the article, what is "the silver lining" about this bill?

The 2,315 page Dodd-Frank financial regulation bill should not be called "financial reform."

Instead, it should be called what for what it is: pages and pages of massively costly, counterproductive, and possibly unconstitutional mandates on nearly every type of business except for those government-sponsored enterprises at the root of the crisis.

While the bill claims to crack down on excesses on Wall Street, its harshest impact will likely be on Main Street businesses that had nothing to do with the crisis.

Untouched Government-Sponsored Enterprises

A front-page *Wall Street Journal* article this week noted that "far from Wall Street, President Barack Obama's financial regulatory overhaul ... will leave tracks across the wide-open landscape of American industry." The *Journal* notes that "the bill will touch storefront check cashiers, city governments, small manufacturers."

But one thing it will leave totally untouched are the government-sponsored enterprises Fannie Mae [Federal National Mortgage Association] and Freddie Mac [Federal Home Loan Mortgage Corporation], which new research by Congress's Financial Crisis Inquiry Commission and other bodies shows was even more of a prime factor in the subprime boom than originally assumed.

The Federal Housing Finance Agency now reports that Fannie and Freddie purchased 40 percent of all private-label subprime securities in 2003 and 2004.

Indeed, according to Edward Pinto, housing scholar and Fannie's former chief credit officer, millions of mortgages to borrowers with credit scores of less than 660, considered by prominent researchers to be the dividing line for subprime loans, had been labeled by Fannie and Freddie as prime going back as early as 1993.

Rather than wait for Congress's own Financial Crisis Inquiry Commission to issue its report in December to examine the role of Fannie and other causes, Congress has instead passed a bill that will not prevent future bubbles and imposes untold costs that will put the country in danger of slipping back into a recession.

New collateral requirements on derivatives could cost U.S. companies as much as $1 trillion in lost capital and liquidity, according to the International Swaps and Deriviatives Association. And as the *Journal* piece notes, these costs would not just hit big banks, but farmers who use derivatives to hedge the price of their crops and fuel for their tractors.

The new Consumer Financial Protection Bureau could also hit retailers that issue credit tangentially related to their business, such as small stores that offer layaway plans.

On the other side of the retail ledger, some of the biggest retailers also got an unjustified mandated benefit with the [U.S. Senator Dick] Durbin amendment that puts price controls on the interchange fees they pay to process credit cards.

This corporate welfare for fat cat merchants will mean higher costs to consumers, community banks, and credit unions.

Exceeding the Limits

In addition, the bill contains provisions that will empower special interests at the expense of ordinary shareholders and that may exceed the limits of the U.S. Constitution.

The bill's "orderly liquidation" authority will allow the Federal Reserve and the Treasury Department not just to bail out firms whose failure is deemed to be a threat to "financial stability," but to actually seize firms that are not even asking for a bailout.

The "proxy access" provisions would override longstanding state rules in corporate director elections and force companies and their shareholders to subsidize director elections by special interest-shareholder, such as unions, enviromentalists and others.

This would give these groups leverage to cut deals with management to push through agenda items, such as the card check abolition of secret ballots in labor election and carbon cap-and-tax reductions, that they can't get through the halls of Congress.

The silver lining is that the more people found out about the potential unintended consequences of this bill, the less popular it became.

The bill cleared cloture with the bare minimum 60 votes that it needed. In the House, almost all Republicans, as well as 19 Democrats voted no on the final bill.

As a result of the growing skepticism of the bill, publicized by the Competitive Enterprise Institute [CEI] and other free-market groups, a few of the most horrific provisions, such as those that would have hurt angel investors and ensnared manufacturers in the definition of "financial companies," were dropped. And one genuinely pro-growth reform was adopted.

That measure, which was added over Chairman [Chris] Dodd and Chairman [Barney] Frank's objections, helps fix costly and counterproductive provisions of the last "financial reform": the Sarbanes-Oxley Act of 2002.

Back Where We Started

After the signing ceremony is over, we still end up roughly where we started—with a wobbly financial system dominated by mega-companies prone to shooting themselves, and therefore us, in the ass. Many of the same banking execs who led us on this merry dance remain camped out on Wall Street. No regulators received their marching orders.

Alain Sherter, "Funny Business:
Why the Financial Reform Bill Has Become a Joke,"
BNET, June 30, 2010. www.bnet.com.

Lack of Prevention

This provision will permanently exempt smaller public companies—those with market valuations of $75 million or less—from the law's section 404(b), the mandate of an audit of a company's "internal controls."

This requirement and the rest of the act did nothing to stop the accounting schemes at companies like Lehman Brothers and Countrywide, but instead frustrated honest entrepreneurs with audits of trivial items like possession of office keys and the number of letters in an employee passwords, and cost the U.S. economy $35 billion a year. See my study, "SOXing It to the Little Guy."

Thanks to this relief, many more smaller companies will be able to afford the cost of going public and get the financing they need to grow into the next Microsoft, Facebook, or Google. That is, if they don't get strangled by the other mounds of red tape in this bill.

In this bill, much arbitrary power is delegated to an army of new regulators. CEI will weigh on the new regulations and educate policy makers to ensure that the true interests of American investors, entrepreneurs, and consumers are represented.

In addition, fresh from our recent Supreme Court victory in getting part of the act declared unconstitutional, we will review the law's many constitutional defects.

> *"While the resulting legislation will not end too-big-to-fail, prevent future bailouts, or significantly rein in risk taking on Wall Street, it is nevertheless worth supporting."*

Even the Gutted Reform Bill Will Provide Meaningful Change

Zach Carter

Zach Carter is the economics editor for AlterNet, an independent media website and a fellow at Campaign for America's Future. In the following viewpoint, Carter claims that the financial reform bill in Congress has been weakened through compromise but is still a good first step toward regulating Wall Street banks. Carter asserts that the bill makes strides toward ensuring consumer protection against banking schemes and regulates derivatives practices that artificially raised prices on gas and food. However, Carter acknowledges that the bill does not curb the growth of big banks, thus more work needs to be done to amend the bill over the next few years.

Zach Carter, "Wall Street Reform: A Good First Step," AlterNet.com, June 25, 2010. Reprinted with permission.

As you read, consider the following questions:

1. Why is Carter pleased that the reform bill calls for an audit of the US Federal Reserve Bank?

2. Who does Carter believe will be tapped to head the new Consumer Financial Protection Bureau?

3. Why does Carter see the final reform bill as a sign of weakness in the Democratic Party?

Members of Congress finished ironing out their differences on Wall Street reform last night [June 24, 2010], and the resulting bill deserves unequivocal support from progressives and conservatives alike. But while the final package is a necessary first step to overhauling the nation's out-of-control financial sector, it will do very little to change the destructive status quo on Wall Street. The bill is a good first step. The public deserves to see stronger reforms from Congress next year.

Reform Takes Time

As a matter of history, sweeping financial change takes several years to secure. It took Franklin Delano Roosevelt seven years to enact all of his New Deal banking regulations, and President Barack Obama appropriately sees the 1930s crisis as the historical analog to today's meltdown-and-reform process. Obama is correct to state that the legislation approved by Congress late last night is the most significant since the Depression—but it is a hollow truth. The U.S. government has been steadily deregulating the banking industry ever since Roosevelt, and the mere act of moving policy in the opposite direction is enough to claim the mantle of dramatic reform. Actually living up to the precedent set by Roosevelt will take several years of serious work, and major legislative action during the next electoral cycle.

Dangerous Compromises

As for the current bill, congressional leaders decided late last night to gut the only two serious structural reforms still on the table. With the political wind at their backs, and the finish line clearly in sight, lawmakers decimated an effort to end outright gambling by the nation's largest banks, and sabotaged a plan to rein in rampant speculation in derivatives—the out-of-control market that brought down AIG and necessitated the bailouts of every major U.S. bank. By adopting the plan from Sen. Blanche Lincoln, D-Ark., to fix derivatives and implement a strong version of the Volcker Rule banning proprietary trading, Congress could have made significant strides toward ending the too-big-to-fail financial oligopoly that held taxpayers hostage in 2008. Instead, Congress chose to reinforce the current destructive banking regime.

But while the resulting legislation will not end too-big-to-fail, prevent future bailouts, or significantly rein in risk taking on Wall Street, it is nevertheless worth supporting. Three important measures made it through that will make the global economy a fairer and more just marketplace. Those three reforms will not be enough to prevent future financial crises, nor will they be able to ameliorate the fallout from those crises once they occur, but they are nevertheless critical.

Auditing the Federal Reserve

First, we will get a thorough audit of the Federal Reserve [the Fed], an agency which has funneled $4 trillion in bailout funding to the nation's financial system without any oversight or transparency. The public will finally know how its money is being spent, and credit is due to Rep. Alan Grayson, D-Fla., Rep. Ron Paul, R-Texas, and Sen. Bernie Sanders, I-Vt., who fought hard for the plan in the face of overwhelming Wall Street lobbying. Kudos are also due to activist journalists Mike Elk and Jane Hamsher, who cobbled together a coalition of good government supporters across the political spectrum and made the Fed audit a centerpiece of the legislative debate. The Fed's blunders on the bailout of AIG have created significant momentum for real reforms, and further information about the secretive agency's operations will help build momentum for next year's financial fights.

Ensuring Consumer Protection

The legislation also includes a critical overhaul of the nation's consumer protection regime wherever banks are concerned. For the first time, the public will have a regulator dedicated to defending consumers against bank abuses, with no other conflicts. The new Consumer Financial Protection Bureau has been pilloried with unnecessary loopholes, but the resulting agency will nevertheless be able to write and enforce meaningful regulations on the financial sector. This is a major accomplishment, made all the more significant by the fact that the front-runner to head the new agency has already established herself as one of the most important voices on U.S. economic policy.

As chair of the oversight panel for the Troubled Asset Relief Program [passed in 2008 to assist the financial sector], Elizabeth Warren has taken a position with extremely limited statutory power and converted it into the only mouthpiece for the American middle class in Washington, D.C. She has done a far better job than even the most optimistic good government activists had hoped for, and giving her free reign to crack down on consumer abuses will be a major victory for the American economy. She has not been formally nominated for the post yet, but the world will be a better place once she is.

Finally, while Lincoln's derivative overhaul was largely destroyed, she did manage to preserve tough new rules regulating both food and gas derivatives. The resulting legislation will not keep Wall Street from gambling with our future, but it will make it much more difficult for financiers to jack up the prices of basic necessities in their quest for bigger bonuses. Back in the spring and summer of 2008, prices for food went through the roof as a result of heavy speculation in market for agricultural derivatives—raw bets placed on the future price of corn, rice and other farm products. The resulting price increases forced consumers the world over to pay too much for food, and sparked outright starvation in regions that could not afford the increases.

The same thing happened with gasoline. Remember paying over $4.00 a gallon? That had nothing to do with the fundamentals of supply and demand—it was a direct result of wild speculation in the market for energy derivatives. The bill approved last night will end that abuse. As a result of Lincoln's efforts, two excesses that created real, tangible hardship for millions of people will be eliminated.

More Work to Do

This bill is unquestionably deserving of support. It will make the global economy a fairer marketplace. But it will not end the too-big-to-fail incentives that encourage Wall Street to take wild risks and stick taxpayers with the tab, nor will it sufficiently overhaul the market that brought down AIG, nor will it end the widespread practice of bigwig bankers gambling with taxpayer money. All of those reforms could have been enacted—explicit, concrete amendments were offered on all three, and congressional leaders rejected them in an overt effort to rake in campaign contributions from Wall Street. Republicans resort to such political calculations all the time— catering to entrenched corporate interests has been their only economic strategy since the [Ronald] Reagan years. But it is enormously disappointing to see significant swaths of the Democratic Party adopt the same strategy (particularly the New Democrats, who should rename themselves the Wall Street Democrats after this episode) and even more frightening to see the Democratic leadership incapable of corralling these turncoats.

So support the Wall Street reform bill: it's a good first step toward building an economy that works for all citizens, not just bankers. But demand that your elected leaders finish the job next year. Too-big-to-fail lives on, and must be defeated.

Editor's Note: The Dodd-Frank Wall Street Reform and Consumer Protection Act was signed into law by President Barack Obama on July 21, 2010.

Periodical and Internet Sources Bibliography

The following articles have been selected to supplement the diverse views presented in this chapter.

Peter Eavis	"New Spin on Derivatives Debate," *Wall Street Journal*, June 16, 2010.
Economist	"The Volcker Rule: Bang or Whimper?" June 24, 2010.
Peter Grier	"Financial Reform Bill: What Does It Do About Firms Deemed 'Too Big to Fail'?" *Christian Science Monitor*, June 25, 2010.
Arthur Levitt	"A Missed Opportunity on Financial Reform," *Wall Street Journal*, June 24, 2010.
New York Times	"The Derivatives Endgame," June 23, 2010.
Charles Scaliger	"Finance Reform," *New American*, May 10, 2010.
Allan Sloan with Doris Burke	"6 Simple Steps to Fix Wall Street," *Washington Post*, May 9, 2010.
James Surowiecki	"Masters of Main Street," *New Yorker*, July 12, 2010.
Meredith Whitney	"The Small Business Credit Crunch," *Wall Street Journal*, May 17, 2010.

For Further Discussion

Chapter 1

1. Mark Gimein argues that Wall Street banks did not cause the mortgage crisis that resulted in national and global recession. He maintains that these big banks only bought up the mortgages transacted by other lending institutions (chiefly on the West Coast) to spread risk—a responsible move, as Gimein insists. Examining the viewpoint by Charles Hurt and David Seifman and any other viewpoints in this anthology, explain whether you think Gimein's assertion is sound. Why do you think the media would choose to pick on Wall Street banks, as Gimein contends? Do you think this critique of the media is fair? Address these questions in your answer.

2. Much of the criticism leveled at the financial reform bill that passed Congress in July 2010 was that it failed to indict the federal mortgage institutions—Fannie Mae (Federal National Mortgage Corporation) and Freddie Mac (Federal Home Loan Mortgage Corporation)—for supposedly contributing to the subprime mortgage craze. Read the viewpoint by Charles W. Calomiris and Peter J. Wallison and the counterpoint by Richard F. Syron (and any other viewpoints in the anthology) and decide whether you think Fannie Mae and Freddie Mac should be shut down or more strictly regulated. In formulating your answer, explain why the government would be hesitant to agree to the termination or regulation of these institutions.

3. After rereading all the viewpoints in this chapter, explain what economic and legislative forces, as well as major participants, led to the financial crisis. In your opinion, does

any one factor stand out as particularly blameworthy, and do you think this factor can and will be remedied by the financial reform bill?

Chapter 2

1. Carl C. Icahn blames the executives of major financial firms for reckless speculation that eventually caused the recent crisis and recession. He believes Congress must rein in these executives by giving more power to shareholders who supposedly would not engage in such risk taking. Do you think the financial collapse was caused by profit-hungry executives? What evidence can you find on the Internet or in other news sources to support this claim? What evidence can you find to suggest Wall Street executives were not acting irresponsibly?

2. Many analysts have condemned the role of the shadow banking system—numerous non-banking, financial institutions that served as middlemen between mortgage lenders and investors worldwide—for contributing to the financial crisis. Stephen Spruiell and Kevin Williamson, for example, claim that these organizations did not keep enough capital on hand to back mortgage trades or clearly outline risks of their trades to borrowers and investors. They claim the government needs to regulate these organizations, which have clear links to major banks yet operate outside federal law. Citing their viewpoint, explain the advantages such regulation would provide. Then, doing further research culled from this anthology or from other news sources, explain the disadvantages that might result from regulation.

3. David M. Mason contends that regulation of the derivatives market will make banks less likely to trade in them, and thus not spread the risks associated with specific markets. According to Mason, banks need these trades to ensure that if markets fail, the shock will be spread to risk-

taking investors instead of being concentrated in banks or other financial institutions whose collapse could severely impact businesses and average clients. Do you agree with this argument? What elements of the argument do you find most persuasive?

4. Simon Johnson and James Kwak insist that big banks have too much influence in the economy and the government. Do you agree with this claim? What evidence can you find to support this conclusion? What do you think should be done to make sure that big banks do not wield too much influence in politics and society?

Chapter 3

1. President Barack Obama was a staunch advocate of the reform bill that passed Congress in July 2010. In his viewpoint in this chapter, Obama argues that the reform bill is necessary because it will curb the excesses of big banks. William P. Hoar, in his counterpoint, claims the reform bill will not stop big banks from risk taking. After examining the evidence in both viewpoints and reading the finalized reform bill (which can be found online), explain whether you think the legislation will keep big banks from gambling with funds. Then, address Hoar's contention that the bill leaves taxpayers open to further bailouts of big banks if their future deals turn sour. Find out to what extent Hoar is correct or incorrect in his assertion.

2. Numerous media pundits and legislators claimed that a reform bill had to ensure that no financial institution was above failure, meaning that all banks had to be held liable for their bad investments and allowed to dissolve if they became insolvent. In his viewpoint, David Zaring makes the unusual claim that too much focus has been placed on "too big to fail" provisions because, in his view, legislators are eager to break up big banks. Using this and any other viewpoints in this anthology, explain whether you

believe legislators might be acting unwisely in trying to carve up big banks or whether such provisions are necessary to prevent another crisis.

3. Examine the opposing pair of viewpoints by Senator Blanche Lincoln and Federal Deposit Insurance Corporation chairperson Sheila C. Bair on the pros and cons of forcing derivatives trading out of banks. What kinds of arguments does each author use to make her point? What are the strengths of each argument? What are the flaws?

4. The final two viewpoints in this chapter acknowledge that the final version of the reform bill passed by Congress was not as strong and comprehensive as earlier drafts and left out some regulations that the authors believed were necessary. Why does Zach Carter claim the bill, though weakened, is still a good first step toward meaningful financial reform? Why does John Berlau believe that it will not change anything? In formulating your answer, be sure to explain what measures (of the various ones articulated in this and previous chapters) you think should have gone into the bill. Also identify which measures that were included will do the most to prevent another crisis.

Organizations to Contact

The editors have compiled the following list of organizations concerned with the issues debated in this book. The descriptions are derived from materials provided by the organizations. All have publications or information available for interested readers. The list was compiled on the date of publication of the present volume; the information provided here may change. Be aware that many organizations take several weeks or longer to respond to inquiries, so allow as much time as possible.

American Enterprise Institute for Public Policy Research (AEI)

1150 Seventeenth Street NW, Washington, DC   20036
(202) 862-5800 • fax: (202) 862-7177
website: www.aei.org

A nonpartisan public policy organization, the American Enterprise Institute for Public Policy Research (AEI) works to promote government policies that espouse the ideals of the free market economy. AEI contends that these policies provide the best opportunity for economic growth and development in the United States. In accordance with these views, AEI opposes government intervention into the private sector and believes that regulation of business limits financial recovery from the ongoing recession. The bimonthly publication of the institute, the *American*, contains detailed articles outlining AEI's stance on the economy and the government's role in helping it grow.

Americans for Financial Reform

1629 K Street NW, 10th Floor, Washington, DC   20006
(202) 466-3311
e-mail: info@ourfinancialsecurity.org
website: www.ourfinancialsecurity.org

A coalition of more than 250 organizations representing consumer, labor, and investor rights among others at the national, state, and local levels, Americans for Financial Reform seeks to enact policy to reform the financial industry in the United States. The organization believes that big banks, credit card companies, and Wall Street insiders have controlled the financial system for too long, and the time has come to impose increased regulation on these entities to help the American people enjoy greater economic security and prosperity. Information about campaigns sponsored by the organization as well as up-to-date information about current legislation can be found on the Americans for Financial Reform website.

Brookings Institution

1775 Massachusetts Avenue NW, Washington, DC   20036
(202) 797-6000
website: www.brookings.edu

The Brookings Institution, a nonprofit, public policy think tank, conducts research and provides policy recommendations that maintain the strength of the American democracy, promote economic growth and prosperity for the American people, and foster international cooperation. The organization has generally supported increased regulation on the financial system to help guard against future recessions; however, it has been skeptical of the efficacy of recently passed legislation, criticizing it for leaving many of the regulatory standards worded vaguely. Detailed information about the Brookings Institution's views on government regulation of the private financial sector can be found on the Brookings website or in the organization's periodic newsletters and e-mail alerts.

Cato Institute

1000 Massachusetts Avenue NW
Washington, DC   20001-5403
(202) 842-0200 • fax: (202) 842-3490
website: www.cato.org

The libertarian Cato Institute was founded in 1977 to advance the ideas of liberty, free market economics, and peace. The organization frowns upon government interference into any and all aspects of American life, on issues ranging from social to economic. Cato has ardently opposed government regulation of Wall Street since the onset of the current recession. Cato's study "Would a Stricter Fed Policy and Financial Regulation Have Averted the Financial Crisis?" answers a resolute "no" to the title question and argues that increased regulation only stifles economic growth and recovery. Additional information about the organization's views on the government's role in the economy can be found online or in publications such as the *Cato Journal,* the quarterly *Cato's Letters,* and the bimonthly *Cato Policy Report.*

Center for American Progress (CAP)

1333 H Street NW, 10th Floor, Washington, DC   20005
(202) 682-1611 • fax: (202) 682-1867
e-mail: progress@americanprogress.org
website: www.americanprogress.org

The progressive Center for American Progress (CAP) opposes traditionally conservative ideals in American politics by employing the tools of modern mass communication to speak to a broad audience. CAP's preferred economic policy focuses on ensuring growth and creating new opportunities so that all Americans can realize the American dream and share in the country's prosperity. The center has called for increased regulation of the financial system and applauds regulatory legislation that protects consumers as well as large banks and financial institutions. Details about CAP's regulatory stance can be found in articles such as "A Last Bid to Protect Wall Street," "Getting Financial Regulation Right," and "Fixing Wall Street, Protecting Main Street."

Center for Economic and Policy Research (CEPR)

1611 Connecticut Avenue NW, Suite 400
Washington, DC   20009
(202) 293-5380 • fax: (202) 588-1356
e-mail: cepr@cepr.net
website: www.cepr.net

The Center for Economic and Policy Research (CEPR) seeks to create a broader understanding of and participation in the democratic process in America by facilitating research on economic and social issues and presenting its findings to US citizens in a concise, comprehensible manner. CEPR supports increased regulation of the financial sector, seeing it as a guard against future financial crises. However, scholars at the center have argued that with regard to the current financial crisis, regulations existed, but the regulators did not impose those regulations strictly enough and these individuals must be held accountable for not enforcing the law. CEPR's website contains articles such as "Making Financial Regulation Work: A Systemic Risk Regulator" and "Fire Failed Regulators: The Best Regulatory Reform."

Federal Reserve System

Twentieth Street and Constitution Avenue NW
Washington, DC   20551
website: www.federalreserve.gov

The Federal Reserve System was founded in 1913 as the central bank of the United States. Congress created the central bank with hopes that it would make the monetary and financial system of the country safer as well as more flexible and secure. During the current recession, some critics have blamed Federal Reserve policy as being a causal factor in the crisis. Information about the Federal Reserve, its current duties, and its mission can be found on its website.

Heritage Foundation

214 Massachusetts Avenue NE, Washington, DC   20002-4999
(202) 546-4400 • fax: (202) 546-8328
e-mail: info@heritage.org
website: www.heritage.org

The conservative public policy think tank, the Heritage Foundation seeks to advance policies that champion the ideas of free enterprise, limited government, individual freedom, traditional American values, and a strong national defense. The foundation opposes government regulations on business, seeing them as a burden on the American economy that limits growth and opportunity. The Heritage Foundation insists that a free market economy will withstand economic downfall, rebound when it does fall, and flourish. Detailed information about its views on regulation of Wall Street can be read on the organization's website.

Institute for Policy Studies (IPS)

1112 Sixteenth Street NW, Suite 600, Washington, DC   20036
(202) 234-9382 • fax: (202) 387-7915
e-mail: info@ips-dc.org
website: www.ips-dc.org

Originally founded as an anti-war and civil rights organization in 1963, the Institute for Policy Studies (IPS) has since shifted its focus, first to human rights in the 1970s and most recently to international peace and justice movements. As the economic situation in the United States has deteriorated in recent years, IPS has refocused its efforts on the recession at home. The institute supports increased regulation of Wall Street and the financial industry as a whole to protect consumers and guard against future recession. Details of its views can be read on the organization's website.

NYSE Euronext

11 Wall Street, New York, NY   10005
(212) 656-3000
website: www.nyse.com

NYSE Euronext, the organization that operates the New York Stock Exchange (NYSE), was created on April 4, 2007, when the NYSE Group Inc. and Euronext N.V. combined to create the world's leading and most liquid stock market. NYSE Euronext facilitates the exchange of more than eight thousand listed issues including cash equities, futures, options, fixed income, and exchange traded products. Information about the current state of the stock market can be found in NYSE Euronext publications such as the quarterly *NYSE Magazine*.

US Securities and Exchange Commission (SEC)

100 F Street NE, Washington, DC   20549
(202) 942-8088
e-mail: publicinfo@sec.gov
website: www.sec.gov

The US Securities and Exchange Commission (SEC) is the agency of the US government charged with protecting investors; maintaining fair, orderly, and efficient markets; and facilitating capital formation. As such, the SEC is responsible for carrying out the regulations imposed on the financial industry by legislation such as the recent Dodd-Frank Wall Street Reform and Consumer Protection Act. Information about the new SEC initiatives required as part of this bill can be found on the SEC's website along with additional information about the regulatory work facilitated by the commission.

Bibliography of Books

William D. Cohan *House of Cards: A Tale of Hubris and Wretched Excess on Wall Street.* New York: Anchor Books, 2010.

Charles Gasparino *The Sellout: How Three Decades of Wall Street Greed and Government Mismanagement Destroyed the Global Financial System.* New York: HarperBusiness, 2009.

Nicole Gelinas *After the Fall: Saving Capitalism from Wall Street—and Washington.* New York: Encounter Books, 2009.

Gary B. Gorton *Slapped by the Invisible Hand: The Panic of 2007.* New York: Oxford University Press, 2010.

Alan C. Greenberg *The Rise and Fall of Bear Stearns.* New York: Simon & Schuster, 2010.

Simon Johnson and James Kwak *13 Bankers: The Wall Street Takeover and the Next Financial Meltdown.* New York: Pantheon Books, 2010.

John Lanchester *I.O.U.: Why Everyone Owes Everyone and No One Can Pay.* New York: Simon & Schuster, 2010.

Randall Lane *The Zeroes: My Misadventures in the Decade Wall Street Went Insane.* New York: Portfolio, 2010.

Michael Lewis *The Big Short: Inside the Doomsday Machine.* New York: W.W. Norton, 2010.

Roger Lowenstein *The End of Wall Street*. New York: Penguin Press, 2010.

Sebastian Mallaby *More Money than God: Hedge Funds and the Making of a New Elite*. New York: Penguin Press, 2010.

Johan Norberg *Financial Fiasco: How America's Infatuation with Homeownership and Easy Money Created the Economic Crisis*. Washington, DC: Cato Institute, 2009.

Scott Patterson *The Quants: How a New Breed of Math Whizzes Conquered Wall Street and Nearly Destroyed It*. New York: Crown, 2010.

Henry M. Paulson Jr. *On the Brink: Inside the Race to Stop the Collapse of the Global Financial System*. New York: Business Plus, 2010.

Robert Pozen *Too Big to Save? How to Fix the U.S. Financial System*. Hoboken, NJ: John Wiley & Sons, 2010.

Barry Ritholtz *Bailout Nation, with New Post-Crisis Update: How Greed and Easy Money Corrupted Wall Street and Shook the World Economy*. Hoboken, NJ: John Wiley & Sons, 2010.

Yves Smith *ECONned: How Unenlightened Self Interest Damaged Democracy and Corrupted Capitalism*. New York: Palgrave Macmillan, 2010.

Andrew Ross Sorkin	*Too Big to Fail: The Inside Story of How Wall Street and Washington Fought to Save the Financial System—and Themselves.* New York: Viking, 2010.
Andrew Spencer	*Tower of Thieves: Inside AIG's Culture of Corporate Greed.* New York: Brick Tower, 2009.
Joseph E. Stiglitz	*Freefall: America, Free Markets, and the Sinking of the World Economy.* New York: W.W. Norton & Co., 2010.
Joseph Tibman	*The Murder of Lehman Brothers: An Insider's Look at the Global Meltdown.* New York: Brick Tower, 2009.
Vicky Ward	*The Devil's Casino: Friendship, Betrayal, and the High-Stakes Games Played Inside Lehman Brothers.* Hoboken, NJ: John Wiley & Sons, 2010.
David Wessel	*In Fed We Trust: Ben Bernanke's War on the Great Panic.* New York: Crown Business, 2009.
Mark T. Williams	*Uncontrolled Risk: The Lessons of Lehman Brothers and How Systemic Risk Can Still Bring Down the World Financial System.* New York: McGraw-Hill, 2010.

| Gregory Zuckerman | *The Greatest Trade Ever: The Behind-the-Scenes Story of How John Paulson Defied Wall Street and Made Financial History.* New York: Broadway Books, 2009. |

Index